CAVENDISH GARDENS
CANADIAN PRACTICAL GUIDES

PONDS
& WATER FEATURES

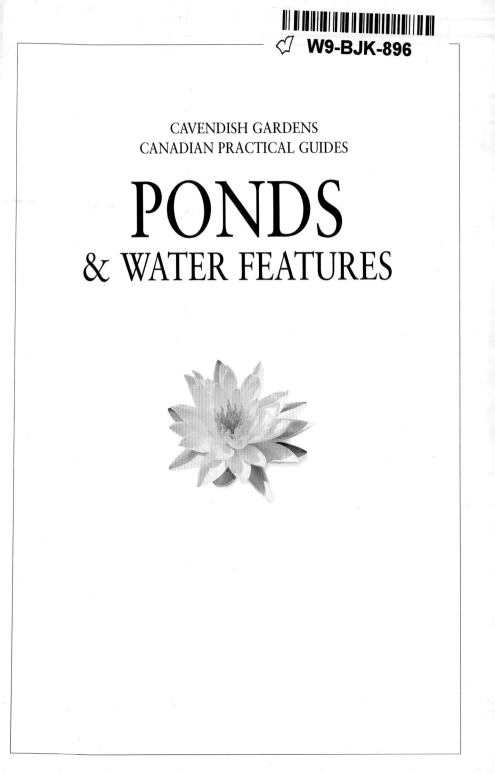

CAVENDISH GARDENS
CANADIAN PRACTICAL GUIDES

PONDS
& WATER FEATURES

PETER ROBINSON

CAVENDISH BOOKS
VANCOUVER

A DK PUBLISHING BOOK
www.dk.com

PROJECT EDITOR Cangy Venables
ART EDITORS Margherita Gianni, Rachael Parfitt

SERIES EDITOR Pamela Brown
SERIES ART EDITOR Stephen Josland
US EDITOR Mary Sutherland

MANAGING EDITOR Louise Abbott
MANAGING ART EDITOR Lee Griffiths

DTP DESIGNER Matthew Greenfield

PICTURE RESEARCHER Mollie Gillard
PRODUCTION MANAGER Patricia Harrington

First Canadian Edition, 1999
2 4 6 8 10 9 7 5 3 1

Published in Canada by
Cavendish Books Inc., Unit 23, 1610 Derwent Way, Delta, BC V3M 6W1
www.gardenbooks.com

Copyright © 1999 Dorling Kindersley Limited, London

A CIP record for this book is available from the National Library, Ottawa

ISBN 1 55289 004 X

Reproduced by Colourscan, Singapore
Printed and bound by Star Standard Industries, Singapore

CONTENTS

DESIGNING WITH WATER

WATER IN THE GARDEN

THROUGHOUT HISTORY WATER has played an important role in gardens all over the world. Its beauty and its cool, refreshing influence have been recognized by almost every culture and society, both in regions where water naturally occurs in abundance and where it is a precious resource. Today, water gardening remains one of the most exciting aspects of garden design.

WATER GARDENING TODAY

One of the most significant developments in the 20th-century water garden has been the breakdown of the traditional distinction between formal and informal design. Designers now freely adapt elements from previous cultures, combining past and present to create unique and innovative styles. Although the average size of garden has decreased, the development of modern materials and techniques has made water gardening far more accessible, enabling features to be built on a small scale.

NATURAL ART
Monet's 19th-century garden at Giverny (above) *combines luxuriant planting with long stretches of water, on which light, shade, and lily pads interplay. This delight in the planting possibilities water offers is echoed in both informal (left) and formal (facing page) gardens today.*

◀ PAINTING WITH PLANTS *A formal setting frames a tapestry of planting in this sunken pool.*

PAST AND PRESENT STYLES

The canals and fountains of Islamic courtly gardens, the precise, spiritually significant placing of rocks and water in Japanese gardens, the magnificent cascades and spouts of the European stately home – all of these demonstrate a historical approach to design in which stone and water were the key elements to be displayed. This is seen today in the cooling jets and sprays that refresh us in modern, architect-designed public spaces. In gardens, however, it is the potential for planting that water offers that is chiefly valued, a trend set in the 19th century and encouraged by factors such as the craze for Chinoiserie, the Impressionist paintings of Monet, and the breeding of new and exquisite waterlilies.

Today, gardeners enjoy a wider choice of beautiful water plants than ever before. A well-planted pond is one of the most popular garden features, and, as city encroaches over countryside, new concerns, such as the desire to provide watery havens for wildlife in our gardens, have influenced

▲ ISLAMIC INFLUENCE
This water feature has incorporated many Moorish elements of design, including decorative stonework, an ornate mask, and restrained planting.

◀ CONTAINER CHARM
A tiny but beautiful, self-contained feature can bring the refreshing sight and sound of water into the smallest space.

design and style. Water conservation is also a key modern issue. Although nothing new in countries with dry climates, where the use of decorative, hard landscaping rather than extensive, water-hungry planting has always been popular, water conservation has led gardeners to a rediscovery of the formal style and the beauties of stone and ornament combined with water. Self-contained features that incorporate no planting at all are not only water-wise but also ideally suited in style to the small gardens that so many of us own today.

A WEALTH OF POSSIBILITIES

Today, garden designers fearlessly assemble formal and informal elements and ornaments influenced by cultures around the world, both traditional in style and eye-catchingly modern, to create highly original water features. With the present availability of excellent, labor-saving materials and techniques, there is no better time to bring the beauties and possibilities of water into your garden.

▲ JAPANESE STYLE
This simple stone lantern, surrounded by clear water and stones, captures the tranquil associations central to Japanese garden design.

▼ MODERN WATER GARDEN
The current trend to synchronize formal geometrical styling with adventurous planting is evident in this contemporary water feature.

FORMAL WATER FEATURES

A FORMAL POOL UTILIZES HARD landscaping materials, whose role is to frame the serenity or the movement and life of the water within. Such features derive their poised looks from regularity of form and line, and symmetry and geometric shapes are strong elements. Squares or rectangles are especially suited to small gardens with preexisting regular features such as paving, fencing, and walls. Restrained planting will complement, rather than dominate, the feature.

HOW FORMAL POOLS ARE MADE

In the past, concrete was the only option for building a formal pool, and although modern advances have made concrete easier to use, it still makes for heavy, time-consuming work. The simplest way to make a formal pool is with a preformed rigid liner (*see pp.16–21*). Once brittle and garish objects, these are now recommended: they are long-lasting, come in neutral colors and in a variety of sizes and regular

ROCKS IN THE ROUND
The outline of this circular pool is accentuated by regular, concentric rings of river rocks, making a tiny pond into an attractive focal point where path and lawn meet.

MAIN ADVANTAGES

• Small ponds have a frame, making them look less "lost" and insignificant.
• Attractive materials can be used to complement existing paving, fencing, or walls.
• Ideal where a raised pool would be attractive or of benefit.
• Sets off architectural or specimen plants.

or smoothly curving shapes. On a small scale, container ponds (*see pp.34–39*) such as half-barrels or troughs make delightful features for a patio or small urban garden. Moving water (*see pp.40–47*) complements the formal style well, even in the simplest displays such as wall-mounted spouts, river rock fountains, and brimming urns.

CHOOSING A STYLE

A formal pool provides an excellent opportunity to use decorative materials. Use edging to complement or contrast with surroundings, both in color and texture. Plant enthusiasts can alternate paving with planting pockets, or place potted plants around a pool.

Styling can echo the past or strike boldly into the future. Classical square pools surrounded by square stone slabs echo the solid design of the Romans, especially when embellished by statuary, whereas a narrow canal is reminiscent of Moorish gardens. Japanese design is governed by a precise placing of plants, water, and rock. Westerners find this meticulous attention to detail difficult to portray and maintain on a large scale, but the use of gravel, Japanese-style ornaments, and materials such as bamboo can create an Oriental niche.

Many gardeners experiment with newer trends such as brickwork painted in bold colors, and mosaics enhanced by one of the striking, modern ornaments and sculptures offered by young designers at garden and craft fairs.

▲ FORMAL SEATING AREA
A raised pool is especially effective when high enough to use wide coping as a casual seat. The big leaves of the rheum look clean and bold against the large stone slabs.

▼ ARCHITECTURAL ELEGANCE
The vertical planting in this canal-like pool is confined to the center to emphasize the clean lines of the pool's edge. The liner is disguised by the stonework used in the side walls.

INFORMAL WATER FEATURES

AN INFORMAL WATER FEATURE should appear naturally placed; careful positioning in relation to other features is essential so that it blends with existing surroundings. An informal pond can be any shape you want, but make it as uncomplicated as possible for a flowing look, avoiding straight lines and sharp angles. Planting can be as adventurous as you wish, and remember that plants surrounding the pond are as important as those in the water.

LINING INFORMAL SHAPES

The greatest recent boon for gardeners wanting an informal pond has been the development of good, long-lasting, and inconspicuous flexible lining materials (*see pp.23–26*). While a rigid liner can be carefully disguised to create an informal look, sizes, shapes, and contours are limited: rigid units slope sharply, but flexible liners allow gradations of depth, enabling, for example, greater areas for marginal planting, or a beach area that gently slopes into the water. Another

alternative is to line a hole with, literally, tons of imported clay (unless you have your own exceptionally heavy clay soil) – a method popular for large landscaping projects but a somewhat daunting undertaking in a domestic setting.

MAIN ADVANTAGES

• Blends well into a naturalistic, informal garden style; can be any shape or size.
• Easy to construct, with the minimum of building materials to buy and install.
• Gives maximum opportunity for planting, with the especial benefit of allowing the rich textural contrasts of moisture-loving plants.
• Can be made attractive to wildlife, providing great benefit to many creatures as well as pleasure to the observer.

SYLVAN SCENE
Ornaments need not look out of place in the informal pond; nymphs are known for their partiality for leafy settings.

DESIGN CONSIDERATIONS

Whereas with a formal pool the object is often to display attractive building materials at the water's edge, the charm of an informal pool lies in well-planted margins that seamlessly disguise the boundary between water and land. Wildlife also appreciates the shelter of dense foliage at the water's edge. You may want to keep a small part of the pond margin edged with hard materials for viewing and for access: you can easily incorporate a small paved platform or, for maximum naturalistic effect, a pebble beach (*see p.31*).

If you are lucky enough to have a natural pond, it will be hard to see where its edges are: moisture-loving plants will colonize the margins, tapping into the rich reserves of available water. But in a lined pond, especially a small one, the point of the liner is to keep the water in, rather than seeping into the surrounding soil. You can add bog gardens (*see p.29*) around the edges, or use skillful associations between marginal and garden plants to blur the point at which poolside planting merges into adjacent beds and borders. These opportunities for imaginative planting reinforce the perennial appeal of the informal pond.

▲ BEST OF BOTH WORLDS
Plants spill over the edges around most of this pond, but one side has been kept clear for an area of paving and an inviting bench.

▼ BOGGY SURROUNDINGS
Lush areas of moisture-rich soil around a pond increase the feature's impact and the possibilities for planting. Natural rocks create promontories and perching places for birds.

MOVING WATER FEATURES

THE VISUAL EXCITEMENT AND REFRESHING sound of moving water can enhance the smallest garden. The main requirement is the need for electricity to drive a circulating pump (*see pp.53–55*) that will push the water back to its source. Low-voltage pumps are submersible, easy to install, and very safe. Apart from occasional cleaning of the strainer, they require little maintenance.

EMBELLISHING PONDS AND POOLS

A fountain (*see p.41*), either gurgling or spouting from the water surface or from a sculpture or ornament, is the classic choice for a formal pool. These need not be centrally placed: water cascading from an ornament such as an urn, jug, or figurine at the side of the pool can be used to enhance both formal and informal features. Even a low-voltage pump will have the capacity to drive water a short distance from the pool, so you can add rocky streamlets and waterfalls in an informal setting, or perhaps, for a pool in a paved area, a regular canal from which a ribbon of water will flow over a level "spill stone" at the pool's edge (*see pp.44–45*).

The air is noticeably cooler and damper in the vicinity of fountains and cascades: not only a refreshing benefit for the gardener but much appreciated by wildlife and by moisture-loving plants.

▶ CASCADING STREAM
Level ground can be gently landscaped to include a small cascade. A waterproof lining is easy to disguise with rocks, stones, and planting.

▼ ELEGANCE AND LIGHT
A terracotta pot overflows with gently trickling water, surrounded by randomly placed rocks. The clean lines are accentuated by the perfection of calla lilies.

SELF-CONTAINED WATER FEATURES

In self-contained features, a modest quantity of water is continually recirculated by means of a small pump, either filling a decorative basin, as with many wall-mounted features (*see p.46*), or a hidden reservoir, as in a river rock or "bubble" fountain (*see p.42*). Plants are usually incidental, although a basin or trough reservoir may have room for one or two specimens. Surrounding plants, however, undoubtedly benefit from the gentle misting of water into the atmosphere from the moving water.

These features, although small and offering limited opportunities for the use of aquatic plants, have many advantages. Their size means that they can be incorporated into the smallest courtyard or even a balcony. Without an open expanse of water, these features are safe for children, and they can be sited in shade. A pool with plants must be positioned in sunlight, or the plants will die and the water become dank

A COOL CORNER
In a shady corner, surrounded by pots of fragrant lilies, an ornamental wall fountain makes an attractive water outlet. Many mask styles and abstract designs are available.

MAIN ADVANTAGES

• Brings sound and movement to the garden, sparkling in sunlight.
• Moving water pumps oxygen and moisture into the air, creating a refreshing atmosphere for people, wildlife, and plants.
• Opportunity to use ornaments and sculpture.
• Self-contained features may be sited in shade, unlike pools and ponds.

and polluted. Similarly, an area of still, standing water will become stagnant in shade. But a self-contained feature with no plants, and in which the water is constantly moving, will remain clean and glistening, making these small features invaluable in small, enclosed spaces where refreshment and a little sparkle is most needed.

MAKING A WATER FEATURE

FORMAL STYLE

REGULARITY IS ALL-IMPORTANT when building a formal pool. Careful attention to measurements, angles, and levels is essential; nothing reveals uneven or sloping edges and paving than a still water surface. Straight sides of the pool must be parallel with each other and the wider surroundings. Think carefully about placement before you choose a position, and consider using a rigid unit, where all the work of checking edges and corners is taken care of for you. All you need to do is to install the unit perfectly level with the ground.

INSTALLING A RIGID POOL UNIT

Ideal for the novice water gardener and non-DIY expert, rigid units are simple to install, easy to clean, and usually come complete with advice on stocking levels. They come in many sizes and colors; dark colors are the least obtrusive. They can be sunk into the ground, or semi-raised (*see p.20*). Lush growth of plants can disguise the lip of a rigid unit, but it is easier to hide it under paving, again making this a good choice for formal styling.

BUYING TIPS
• Fiberglass units are strong and are especially recommended for raised pools; cheaper plastic units are less durable but can be used for short-lived sunken ponds.
• Units without 10–12in/25–30cm wide marginal shelves restrict planting possibilities.
• Units always look smaller after they have been installed and edged, so overestimate the size of unit that you require. Mark out on the site the size you intend buying first, to check.

▼ COPING WITH SLOPES
A slope (below) is undesirable and should be leveled (below right), or a strong retaining wall constructed to support and conceal the exposed unit.

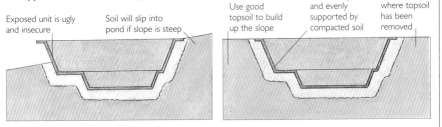

Exposed unit is ugly and insecure

Soil will slip into pond if slope is steep

Use good topsoil to build up the slope

Unit strongly and evenly supported by compacted soil

Replenish planting areas where topsoil has been removed

◄ FRAMED MIRROR *Regular paving overhangs the pool edges, defining an expanse of clear water.*

YOU NEED:

TOOLS
- Bamboo stakes
- Wooden pegs
- String
- Spade
- Plastic sheet or wheelbarrow
- Straightedge
- Carpenter's level
- Tape measure
- Bricklayer's trowel

MATERIALS
- Soft sand for a 2in/5cm layer over base of excavation (ask your supplier to advise for your unit)
- Rigid unit, here 6½x6½ft/2x2m
- Choice of edging: here, 20 paving slabs, 18x18in/ 45x45cm
- ½ cu yd/200kg of crushed stone
- 4 50lb/25kg bags of ready-mix mortar

MARKING OUT THE SHAPE

1 If the unit is symmetrical, you can simply turn it upside down and mark its outline directly on the ground. If not, or if the unit has an offset deep zone, place stakes at each corner, making sure that these are parallel to the edge of the unit.

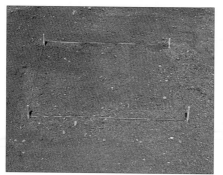

2 Remove the unit and replace the stakes with wooden pegs. Attach string to one of the pegs, then wind and loop it around the others to form a shape that represents the outline of the lip of the unit.

DIGGING THE SHALLOW ZONE

1 With the spade, mark an outline 6–10in/ 15–25cm outside the string guide. This will allow plenty of space for backfilling later, which is necessary to secure the sides of the unit firmly with compacted surrounding soil.

2 Measure the depth of the unit from the rim to the bottom of the marginal shelf with a tape measure and level. Then dig out the hole to the correct depth. This shallow zone will accommodate the marginal shelf.

3 Check that the depth of the hole is uniform by laying a straightedge across it; then measure down with a tape measure, working your way across the hole's width.

4 Remove any stones or sharp objects from the base and sides of the hole; these may scratch or crack the unit. Then firm and level the surface by tamping the ground underfoot.

DIGGING OUT THE DEEPER ZONE

1 Mark out the outline of the deeper zone by putting the unit in position and pressing down firmly so that it leaves an imprint on the soil. Measure the depth and dig out a sloping-sided hole, remembering to allow an extra 2in/5cm for a layer of soft sand; this will cushion the base of the unit.

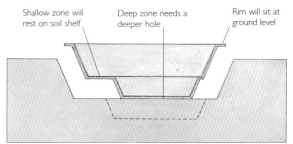

Shallow zone will rest on soil shelf

Deep zone needs a deeper hole

Rim will sit at ground level

2 Dig to the correct depth, then remove any sharp stones from the bottom of the excavation. Add a 2in/5cm layer of soft sand all over the base and side surfaces of the hole. Wetting the sand helps it adhere to the sides.

3 Place the unit in the hole, then use a level and straightedge to check that it is level. Add or remove sand until the deep zone fits snugly and the lip is flush with the ground. Fill partly with water to settle the unit.

BACKFILLING & TAMPING

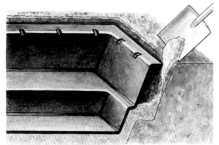

1 **Gradually shovel sand** into the gap between the unit and the excavation wall. You may need to scoop or rake soil away from the rim so that it cannot slip back in.

2 **Use a short length** of wood to tamp sand down firmly all around the unit. Do this at regular intervals as you backfill so that the unit stays level and becomes absolutely secure.

EDGING WITH SLABS

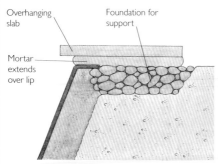

Overhanging slab

Foundation for support

Mortar extends over lip

1 **For a paved edge,** scoop away a 2½in/6cm-deep trench all around the unit, to the width of your slabs, and fill with a layer of crushed stone, making sure to pack some under the lip.

2 **Mortar down slabs** around the pond, with a 2in/5cm overhang over the lip of the unit to conceal it. Use whole slabs in the corners and cut intervening ones, if necessary.

SUPPORTING AND EDGING A SEMI-RAISED POOL UNIT

Rigid pool units can also be used as semi-raised pools, provided the sides are given strong support, which will take some building skill. Soil will provide sufficient protection for the deep zone, but the shallow zone can be given support by a wall of concrete blocks on a concrete footing. With the rim held securely under the coping, the gap (*below*) can be left clear or, in cold climates, filled with insulating polystyrene blocks or ceiling tiles.

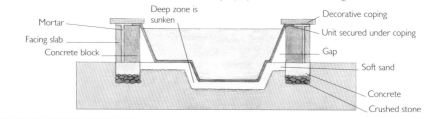

Mortar

Facing slab

Concrete block

Deep zone is sunken

Decorative coping

Unit secured under coping

Gap

Soft sand

Concrete

Crushed stone

PLANTS FOR FORMAL POOLS

Formal ponds are not designed to emulate nature, making them an ideal vehicle for specimen and architectural plants, whose leaves and shape will look even more pronounced when reflected in water. Cool greens, blues, and white create the most restful atmosphere. To stop vigorous plants from taking over, use planting baskets (*see p.56*) to restrict their growth.

USING VERTICAL AND HORIZONTAL PLANES

This attractive formal pool, complemented by exquisite but restrained planting, has transformed a small courtyard garden. The vertical planting of swordlike irises and the spikes of typha enhance the clean-cut lines of the paving and still water surface, while the lily pads soften the symmetrical paving stones and compliment the curved contours of the Ali Baba pot. A unified color scheme and the repeated use of a small collection of plants prevents a fussy look and ties the planting design together.

ADDING HEIGHT
Architectural interest is provided by the vertical lines of Typha latifolia *'Variegata'*

SURFACE COLOR
The deep red flowers of Nymphaea *'Froebelii' add color and elegance.*

PLANTS FOR FORMAL POOLS

MARGINALS	SMALL WATERLILIES
Calla palustris	*Nymphaea* 'Aurora'
Cyperus longus	N. 'Gonnère'
Iris laevigata	N x *helvola*
Iris pseudacorus 'Variegata'	N. 'James Brydon'
Juncus effusus 'Spiralis'	N. 'Laydekeri Fulgens'
Pontederia cordata	N. 'Lucida'
Typha minima	N. 'William Falconer'
Zantedeschia aethiopica	

PLANTING DEPTHS

Most rigid units have a shallow and deeper zone, enabling you to introduce both marginal and deep-water plants to your pond. The shelf space should be wide enough to hold containers housing the marginal plants, while deep-water plants such as waterlilies will enjoy the full depth of the pond. While young waterlilies need shallower water, stand them on a stack of bricks.

Marginal iris

Waterlily in deep zone

INFORMAL STYLE

F LEXIBLE LINER IS THE IDEAL CHOICE for creating informally shaped ponds, perhaps incorporating shallow beach areas and boggy surrounds, and planted to encourage wildlife. To make an informal pond look natural and blend in well with the garden, creative planting at the pond edges is crucial. By selecting plants that go well together in and out of the water (*see p.27*), you can create a seamless transition between the pond and its surrounding planting areas.

MAKING A FLEXIBLE-LINER POND

Various grades of flexible liner are available: polyethylene is inexpensive but liable to tear, and it also becomes brittle and cracks if exposed to sunlight, so if you want a long-lasting feature, it is well worth investing in more expensive butyl, PVC, or EPDM. To protect your investment, always use an underlay fabric, soft sand, insulation, or even old synthetic carpet under the liner. Before buying your liner, work out how large a sheet you need (*see right*), remembering to allow extra if you want to incorporate features such as boggy areas or a beach (*see pp.29–31*).

A good-quality butyl liner can weigh as much as 2lb per sq yd/1kg per sq m, so you may need some help to lay it. If you can unroll it and lay it flat in the sun for half an hour or so, the warmth will make it more

PRACTICAL TIPS

• To calculate the size of liner, take the length and width of the proposed pond, then add twice the depth to each measurement, then add another 20in/50cm or so for edging.
• Steep sides will stretch the liner once the pond is full of water and make it more vulnerable to tearing; gentle slopes and marginal shelf areas reduce the strain.

flexible and easier to mold to the hole's contours. (Roll it up again and carry it to the pond; if you drag it, it may tear.) While you can landscape the pond floor to create different planting depths (*see pp.32–33*), try to keep general outlines simple. You can sod or plant all around the pond, or add a small, informal paved platform at one side (*see p.26*) as a viewing and access point.

MARKING OUT
Even with an informal pond, a level surround is important, or the liner may be difficult to hide. Use marker pegs and a level when digging to make sure the pond edges are not only even but completely horizontal.

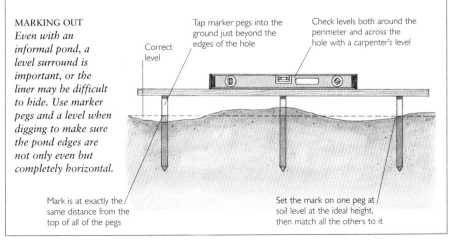

Tap marker pegs into the ground just beyond the edges of the hole

Check levels both around the perimeter and across the hole with a carpenter's level

Correct level

Mark is at exactly the same distance from the top of all of the pegs

Set the mark on one peg at soil level at the ideal height, then match all the others to it

◀NATURAL LOOK *Black flexible lining material is hard to see once the pond is planted.*

YOU NEED:

TOOLS
• Marker pegs
• Club hammer
• Carpenter's level
• Straightedge • Rake
• Spade and shovel
• Bricks to hold liner temporarily in place

MATERIALS
This pond is approx. 10ftx6ft/3mx2m, with a maximum depth of 24–26in/60–65cm.
• ½cu yd/0.5cu m soft sand
• 16x13ft/5x4m underlay
• 16x13ft/5x4m flexible liner
• 25–30 12in/30cm squares of turf, halved, to make soil banks

MARKING AND DIGGING

1 **Mark the outline of the pond** with soft sand (*see inset*). Place one marker peg on this guide to set the ideal level (*see p.23*). Position the remaining pegs at regular intervals around the outline. Use a level and straightedge to make sure they are level.

2 **Make a shallow trench** 2in/5cm deep and 12in/30cm wide around the pond edge. Dig out the hole to 8in/20cm deep. Reserve this useful topsoil. Rake the base and remove any stones; outline the deep zone with sand. Leave marginal shelf areas about 12in/30cm wide.

3 **Excavate the marked area** by another 18–20in/45–50cm. Discard this soil. Rake the base of the hole; remove any sharp stones. Then spread a 1in/2.5cm layer of soft sand over the base of the excavation, where the water pressure will be greatest. Remove pegs.

INSTALLING UNDERLAY AND LINER

1 **Remove any stones** from the sides of the hole and pat the sides flat, then drape the underlay over the excavation. Press it firmly over and into the contours of the hole.

2 **Lift the roll of liner into position** across the hole and unroll it. Be sure not to stretch the fabric; this will reduce its elasticity, and it may be punctured by sharp objects.

3 **Continue to unroll** the liner until it is draped in position. Leave ample overlap around the sides and fold in the creases before filling with water.

4 **Use bricks to hold** the liner temporarily in place, and slowly fill the pond. Let the increasing weight of water pull the liner gently down, moving bricks outward as necessary.

LINING DIFFICULT CORNERS

You will probably have to pleat the liner around sharper curves in informal ponds, particularly where there is also marginal shelving. Careful folding can make the creases look less conspicuous. Once the pond is filled, the weight of water should hold the folds down. Pleated material can also be secured with waterproof tape. Make pleats and folds generous, so that the liner will not be stretched too much. Always fold and tuck in the liner as best you can before filling the pond: the sheer weight of water afterward will make further manipulation difficult.

▲ PLEATING
Use stones to hold the liner as you pleat around curves.

▲ TUCKING IN
Tuck surplus under: the weight of water will hold pleats down.

PREPARING FOR EDGING

1 **Once the pond has filled** to within 2in/5cm of the top of the hole, remove the bricks and let the pond stand for a few hours so that the liner can settle completely into the hole.

2 **Trim off surplus liner** and underlay, leaving an overlap of about 4in/10cm. Keep some trimmings in case you need them for patching repairs in the future (*see p.61*).

MAKING A PLANTING EDGE

Lay two overlapping layers of sod, face down, around the edge of the pond, and add topsoil from the excavation behind them, hiding the liner.

Inverted sod on top of the liner stops soil from falling in

Creeping roots will soon consolidate the soil

▶ CONSOLIDATING THE EDGE
The matted sod makes a fairly solid edge that will be made stronger once the roots of poolside plants grow into them. Do not walk on the edge until plants are established.

LAYING A PAVED PLATFORM

1 **For a simple edging,** mortar rounded or flat stones directly onto the liner, overlapping the pond. You will need to lay a foundation for more formal paving (*see p.20*).

2 **Flat slabs should** overhang the pond by about 2in/5cm to conceal the liner. Do not drop mortar into the water, or you will have to empty the pond, clean, and refill.

PLANTING INFORMAL PONDS

Choosing plants for their flower color is only half the story when planting in and around an informal pond. Plenty of foliage plants are essential to give a lush effect and contrast cool shades of green.

Plantings will look more effective and "planned" if they contain associations of complementary colors, shapes, and textures. See *Plants for Water Features* (*pp.63–77*) to help with your choice.

PLANT ASSOCIATIONS

Even when the area surrounding a lined pond looks natural, pleasing associations between plants in and out of the water can be created. Prostrate conifers (*right*) echo the waving stems of pond weeds, and also complement weathered stone, with a hint of Oriental style. Use vertical-accent plants such as grasses and iris, too, to match plant silhouettes and foliage shapes within the pond and on dry land. Their reflections in the water will enhance the effect.

▲ EDGING SEDGE
Different types of
Carex *can be used in*
and out of the water.

▲ SHOW OF STRIPES
This Phragmites *will*
complement iris with
variegated leaves.

MIRRORING PLANTS

• Use hostas around the pool to echo the wide leaf blades of *Pontederia* and *Sagittaria*.
• Yellow globeflowers (*Trollius*) on banks pick up the flower shape and color of yellow pond lilies (*Nuphar*) and water fringe (*Nymphoides*).
• The rounded leaves of frogbit (*Hydrocharis morsus-ranae*) can be matched by those of creeping Jenny (*Lysimachia*) on dry land.
• Many waterlilies have bronzed or purple-flecked leaves: set them off with dark-foliaged perennials such as *Lobelia* 'Bee's Flame', *Ajuga reptans* 'Burgundy Glow', and *Cimicifuga*.

LAYERED PLANTINGS

Think of the marginal shelves and banks of ponds as terracing, providing an opportunity to create layered planting compositions of increasing height. This works especially well with ponds that are principally viewed from one side, allowing you to create a theater of planting interest. The use of plants with vertical leaf blades (*right*) could be continued with a backdrop of tall grasses and bamboos, with the added benefit of providing shelter for the pond without creating too much shade.

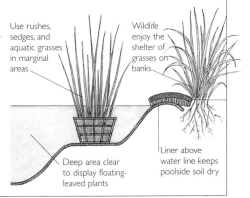

Use rushes, sedges, and aquatic grasses in marginal areas

Wildlife enjoy the shelter of grasses on banks

Deep area clear to display floating-leaved plants

Liner above water line keeps poolside soil dry

BOGS AND BEACHES

WHEREAS RIGID, PREFORMED POOL UNITS have steep sides, using flexible lining material enables you to add features such as gently sloping beaches and shallow boggy areas around pond margins. This not only enhances the natural, informal look of a pond but also provides an ideal environment for attracting wildlife, letting birds approach the water to bathe and giving amphibious creatures damp, well-planted areas around the pond in which to shelter.

MAKING A BOG GARDEN

You can extend the area in which you can grow moisture-loving plants without creating problems of water loss from a pond in two ways: either by buying a large-enough sheet of liner to take it up above ground level and back under again to line a bowl-shaped bog garden filled with soil by the pond, or by lining a hole dug by the pond's edge with less expensive polyethylene (*see overleaf*). Overlapping sheets rather than a single piece of lining are perfectly adequate, since the lining of the bog garden must have some holes poked in it anyway to allow a little drainage, or the waterlogged soil will become stagnant and sour. Since in either

PRACTICAL TIPS
• A bog garden must have a minimum depth of 16–18in/40–45cm, otherwise it will dry out too quickly and will not be water efficient.
• Disguise humps of liner above ground level that form a barrier between pond and bog area by mortaring on stones (*as below*).
• Seep- or trickle hose buried in a bog garden makes watering easy.

case this area of soil is deliberately completely separate from the pond, it must be independently and regularly supplied with water in order to prevent plants from "wicking" out the water.

EXTENDING FLEXIBLE LINER
The hosta and ligularia beyond the pool margins on the left must be watered independently and regularly, since some drainage is essential to prevent waterlogging.

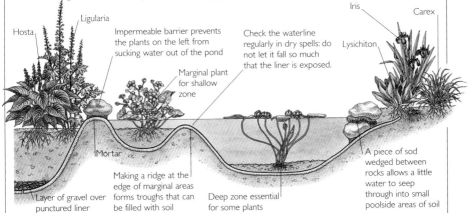

Hosta

Ligularia

Iris

Carex

Impermeable barrier prevents the plants on the left from sucking water out of the pond

Check the waterline regularly in dry spells: do not let it fall so much that the liner is exposed.

Lysichiton

Marginal plant for shallow zone

Mortar

A piece of sod wedged between rocks allows a little water to seep through into small poolside areas of soil

Layer of gravel over punctured liner

Making a ridge at the edge of marginal areas forms troughs that can be filled with soil

Deep zone essential for some plants

◀ BOG PLANTS *A boggy area presents an opportunity for lush planting in even the driest gardens.*

YOU NEED:

TOOLS
- Spade
- Rake
- Garden fork
- Knife or scissors

MATERIALS
For a bog garden approx. 6½ft/2m across:
- 11x11ft/3.5x3.5m heavy-duty polyethylene sheeting
- ½cu yd/0.5cu m pea gravel

(Ask your supplier for advice on quantities for other sizes.)

LINING AN INDEPENDENT BOG GARDEN

1 **Mark out the required shape** and dig a hole about 2ft/60cm deep, with sloping sides. Keep the topsoil for replacement. Rake the area and remove sharp stones.

2 **Drape the lining material** loosely over the hole and press it into the contours. Hold it down with bricks or stones while you make drainage holes with a fork.

FILLING WITH GRAVEL AND SOIL

3 **Spread a 2in/5cm layer of** pea gravel over the sheet with a garden rake. This aids drainage, so that the water does not become stagnant.

4 **Refill with soil.** Before the soil reaches the top, remove the bricks and trim off any surplus liner. Tamp the soil to firm, and water thoroughly. (If you want to incorporate seephose for watering, embed it in the gravel layer, with the buried end blocked. Fit the end above ground with a hose connector.)

▶ FINISHED PLANTING
Moisture-loving plants such as (from left) candelabra primulas, rheums, marsh marigolds (Caltha), and ferns will thrive provided that the soil is always kept damp. Bury the edges of the liner to conceal them.

MAKING A BEACH

A simple, sloping beach makes an inexpensive, appealing addition to a pond and is a real attraction for wildlife. Provided that there is some planting to give them shelter and make them feel safe, amphibious creatures will bask on it, and birds and small mammals will be able to approach the water to drink and bathe. Plan in a beach at the design stage of your pond, so that you can allow for it when buying or ordering your liner.

CREATING A NATURAL LOOK

Use only smooth, washed stones, since sharp edges may damage the liner. Use stones of random sizes, with some half-in and half-out of the water as perching and basking platforms. By combining pebbles with rocks and larger stones, placing the smaller stones nearer the water, you can imitate nature closely. Try to choose stones that match the colors and textures of stones that occur naturally in your garden and of other hard landscaping materials. Leave spaces between large stones at the pond edges as planting pockets.

▶ GRADUATED SLOPE
This informal pond is approached by a graded pebble beach. There is plenty of room for lush planting between the stones, creating welcome cover for wildlife.

HOW IT WORKS

At the edge of the pond excavation, make a shallow shelf sloping down to the water. You must be sure that you have enough liner to cover the beach entirely, or the water will leak out of the pond. Once the underlay and liner are laid, mortar rocks onto the beach area, then fill in with smaller pebbles and gravel. The mortared stones will stop the rest from sliding into the water. Use larger stones at the top of the beach to cover the edge of the liner.

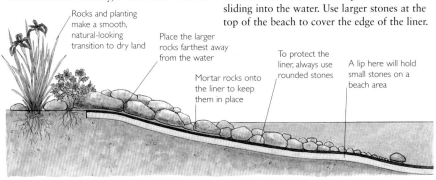

Rocks and planting make a smooth, natural-looking transition to dry land

Place the larger rocks farthest away from the water

Mortar rocks onto the liner to keep them in place

To protect the liner, always use rounded stones

A lip here will hold small stones on a beach area

MAXIMIZING PLANTING POSSIBILITIES

Imaginative landscaping of the pond floor and margins, creating different planting depths, gives the widest opportunities for using the full range of aquatic and poolside plants. A well-planted pond will have maximum appeal to wildlife, especially when native plants and wildflowers are used, providing creatures with their preferred foods as well as water and shelter.

THE PRACTICALITIES OF LANDSCAPING

While the margins of the pond can be shaped and contoured to create whatever effects you desire (*as below*), it is essential to incorporate a central deep zone: it suits many lovely plants, provides shelter and breeding areas for aquatic creatures, and most importantly, guarantees that the pond has a sufficient volume of water to prevent wild variations in temperature.

A substantial body of water deeper than 12in/30cm will very rarely heat up under the sun to temperatures dangerous to plant and animal life, nor freeze solid in winter.

▶ ACHIEVING A BALANCE
Let plants work with, not overwhelm, your pond so that attractive materials at the water's edge and the water surface itself can be seen.

Most waterlilies prefer to be sited where they can enjoy the full depth of the pond

A trough of soil in the deep zone allows pond weeds to root, their stems supported by the water

Large plants will wick out water over liner edges so regular refilling may be needed

Check levels in hot, dry spells to be sure that plants in small, boggy pockets around the pool do not become cut off from the water they need

Plants in baskets can be repositioned to fill gaps

USING DIFFERENT PLANTING DEPTHS AND LEVELS

To make sure that your pond stays healthy, you must first pick some functional plants for the central, open expanse of deep water: submerged plants to contribute oxygen, and floating-leaved plants to give some shade (*see also p.51*). Although useful, these plants can also be decorative – waterlilies being the most obvious example. Once these are planned in, there is a large range of marginal and moisture-loving plants to choose from to create a frame for the water. For a naturalistic look, use plenty of plants, but remember that aquatic and moisture-loving plants grow quickly and vigorously. Planting baskets will help keep them in check, but regular thinning and division (*see pp.59–60*) is essential to prevent overcrowding and keep plants flowering well. The larger your pond, the less frequently you will have to disrupt its environmental balance to lift, divide and replace plants, thin weeds, and scoop up bottom silt. In a large pond, as below, you could incorporate some permanent soil-filled trenches and beds for plants, allowing them to spread and mingle more freely.

FLOATING PLANTS
Waterlilies (see p.66), such as 'Escarboucle', are the most popular plants for deep water. Choose from smaller or more vigorous types to match the size of your pond.

MARGINAL ZONES
Marginal plants (see pp.70–73) that enjoy shallow water or boggy soil, such as Caltha palustris, *play a key role in softening the hard edges of the pond.*

BEYOND THE MARGINS
There are many moisture-loving plants (see pp.74–77), such as the fern Matteuccia struthiopteris, *to complement plants in and around the water.*

Stones mortared onto the liner will provide crevices where floating and oxygenating plants may lightly root to soften less densely planted pond margins

Free-floating plants such as *Pistia stratiotes* will drift informally over the surface

Rock garden plants and alpines will grow in dry planting pockets between rocks

A soil-filled brick bed makes a permanent home for deep-water plants in large wildlife ponds

Brick plinths allow younger and less vigorous deep-water plants to reach the surface

In beds around the pond that do not benefit from the water within it, improve the moisture-retentiveness of the soil by adding plenty of organic matter, use mulches to keep moisture in, and water young plants regularly until established

CONTAINER PONDS

CONTAINERS MAKE WATER GARDENING possible in tiny spaces: on roof terraces, patios, verandas, even in conservatories. A mini-pond under glass can allow you to grow plants that would not survive in your climate outdoors. You can use almost any type of container as long as it is watertight, provided that it is large enough to give plants sufficient depth of water and to guarantee that the water temperature does not fluctuate too wildly in hot weather.

MAKING A SUNKEN MINI-POND

Sinking a container into the ground keeps the water cool in summer and gives some protection from freezing in winter, which can be a problem for exposed containers. It also allows you to use an unattractive and inexpensive container. With thoughtful planting in and around it, you can make this mini-water feature appear much bigger than it really is. You could add small, lined bog gardens around it (*see p.30*) or use attractive edging materials like pebbles.

YOU NEED:

TOOLS
• Spade and trowel
• Straightedge
• Carpenter's level

MATERIALS
• Plastic tub
• Here, edging of 88lb/40kg stones, 110lb/50kg gravel, slabs, and a bag of ready-mix mortar

MARKING AND DIGGING

1 **Place the tub** on the ground. Allowing an extra 2in/5cm for infilling, mark out a ring around the tub with your trowel. Then remove the tub and measure its depth.

2 **With a spade,** dig a hole to the required shape. If the soil is crumbly, stand as far away from the hole as possible to prevent the sides from caving in.

3 **Try the tub** in the hole at regular intervals as you dig until you have reached the correct depth. Once the tub is flush with ground level, insert it into the hole.

◀ PLANTED UP *A container pond can hold several plants, provided that they are regularly divided.*

LEVELING AND BACKFILLING

1 **Lay a straightedge** across the top and use a level to check that the tub is horizontal. This is important: if the hole is uneven, part of the container may be exposed, spoiling the look of your pond.

2 **Shovel soil** into the gap around the container. Work gradually around the tub, tamping the soil down firmly around it with the end of the straightedge to make the tub completely stable and flush with the ground.

MAKING A STONE EDGING

1 **Spread a thin** layer of ready-mix mortar at the edge of the pond. Rather than covering the entire area in one go, do this in stages. Press stones firmly onto the mortar, making sure that the stones slightly overhang the edge of the tub (*see inset*) so that the rim of the container is not visible. Work around the tub until its rim is completely hidden by the stones.

2 **Mortar down a** second circle of stones around the container; you can either grade the stones according to size or arrange them randomly. Once these are attached, more stones or pebbles can be spread onto the ground around them, without mortaring.

STYLING AND PLANTING THE EDGES

1 **Arrange a few flat** irregular slabs in the area around the stones. Butting two or three up together will create stepping stones from which to view the pond and tend plants. Set water plants in the pool, standing marginals in their baskets on stacks of bricks so that they are at the correct height. Young waterlilies may need temporary plinths of bricks, so that the new shoots can reach the surface easily. Arrange the other plants around the pool.

2 **Plant the** surrounding plants, and water in well. Arrange more stones around them until you have a pleasing effect, then fill in with a layer of gravel. The use of decorative mulch should suppress weeds and, more importantly, helps keep the soil cool and damp for moisture-loving plants such as ferns. Water the plants regularly in their first season to help them establish.

PLANTS USED

WATER PLANTS

Waterlily: *Nymphaea* 'Froebelii'
Oxygenator: *Myriophyllum aquaticum*
Vertical accent plant (in basket resting on stack of bricks): *Iris laevigata* 'Variegata'

EDGING PLANTS

Digitalis grandiflora
Iris 'Arctic Fancy'
Iris 'Banbury Beauty'
Lysimachia punctata 'Aurea'

Ferns:
Dryopteris affinis
Dryopteris wallichiana
Grasses:
Molinia caerulea
Phalaris arundinacea 'Picta'

OTHER IDEAS FOR CONTAINER PONDS

Glazed ceramic pots and urns (with any drainage holes stopped up) and galvanized metal tubs make striking container pools, with light glinting from the surfaces of the container and the water. However, pots must not be left outside where cold weather can harm them. Half-barrels make lovely miniature ponds. They can be freestanding, surrounded by plants and perhaps a few stones, or partially or completely sunk into the ground.

WATERPROOFING BARRELS

When barrels are filled with liquid, their wooden staves swell to seal them, so new, well-made barrels should be watertight. However, old barrels and the half-barrel-style planters intended to hold soil may leak and endanger aquatic plants.

Waterproofing with a commercial sealant (your supplier will be able to recommend something suitable) or lining with polyethylene will prevent leaks and prevent residues in old, used barrels from seeping into the water and altering its chemistry.

◄LINING A BARREL
Use galvanized nails or staples to tack the polyethylene around the rim of the barrel, then trim off the surplus. Use bushy or trailing plants around the edges of the barrel to disguise the lining.

◄SEALING WOOD
Paint right up to the rim with a commercial sealant. Let it dry thoroughly but, before you buy plants, fill it with water and allow to stand for a while, to check that it is watertight.

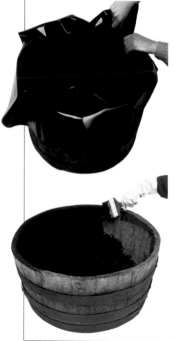

WATER PLANTS FOR CONTAINERS

Your container should be able to accommodate two or three planting baskets, and you can fill in with floating plants. Vertical plants with linear leaves such as iris, rushes, and sedges take up the least room, leaving space for a floating-leaved plant such as a small waterlily, or a free-floating plant such as frogbit. Divide regularly (*see pp.59–60*) to restrain growth.

COPING WITH CLIMATE

If you cannot leave the container outdoors in winter and have nowhere else to keep it or the plants, you will have to restock each spring, although the rhizomes of waterlilies and irises can be stored in cool, moist sand over winter, once they have died down. With a conservatory or greenhouse, overwintering in cool climates is no problem; you can also experiment with some of the more exotic, tender water plants.

COLD WINTERS
Cold will not kill dormant hardy plants, but they will die if the water freezes solid.

UNDER COVER
A container water garden makes an exotic focal point in a conservatory.

VARYING PLANTING DEPTHS
Create different planting depths with bricks to suit a variety of plants. Submerged, or oxygenating, plants will fend for themselves floating free.

Marginals on brick plinths

Waterlilies need the full depth of the tub

Free-floaters do not take up floor space

SUITABLE PLANTS

SMALL PLANTS

Hydrocharis morsus-ranae Frogbit, free-floating
Iris ensata Less vigorous than other water irises
Juncus effusus 'Spiralis' Unusual corkscrew rush
Nymphaea 'Froebelii', *N.* 'James Brydon', *N.* 'Laydekeri Fulgens' Red-flowered waterlilies
Nymphaea 'Odorata Sulphurea Grandiflora', *N.* x *helvola* Yellow-flowered waterlilies
Typha minima Cattail

LESS HARDY PLANTS

Pistia stratiotes Water lettuce, free-floating
Eichhornia crassipes Water hyacinth, free-floating
Salvia auriculata Free-floating fern
Myriophyllum aquaticum Feathery water weed
Nymphaea capensis, *N.* 'Blue Beauty' Unusual blue-flowered waterlilies

See *Plants for Water Features (pp.63–77)* for details. Plants need regular care to stop them from overwhelming each other.

MOVING WATER FEATURES

MOVING WATER BRINGS SOUND AND SPARKLE even in the smallest spaces and can be added in so many ways, from the simplest fountain kit in a pool or in ornamental stonework (*see overleaf*) to building your own, tailor-made cascade or canal. In built-up areas, however, be considerate of others when installing a moving water feature – a neighbor sensitive to noise may be highly annoyed by the splashing you find so relaxing, especially if left on at night.

ADDING A SIMPLE FOUNTAIN

A small, submersible pump (*see p.54*) is all you need to add a fountain to your pond, bringing movement and life and, as a bonus, oxygenating the water and thus helping to keep it healthy. Provided that the jet is no higher than half the width of the pool, water will not escape its margins. There will be an inevitable loss of water as it dissipates and evaporates in the air, so be prepared to top up when necessary (tap water is fine for this). The finer the spray, the more water will be lost. To keep it to a minimum, choose a geyser-type nozzle, which produces a bubbling column or foaming plume of water, rather than a wide-arcing fine spray.

HOW IT WORKS

A standard fountain kit consists of a pump, a rigid pipe, and a nozzle; the pump drives the water up through the head of the fountain, creating a spray pattern. A flow adjuster controls the height and width of spray. For spray heights of up to 4ft/1.2m, install a submersible pump. For anything higher than this, you may need a high-head exterior pump and installation by a qualified electrician.

▼ PLANTS AND MOVING WATER
Many plants, especially waterlilies, dislike moving water, so you need to take care in choosing and positioning them with a fountain or cascade.

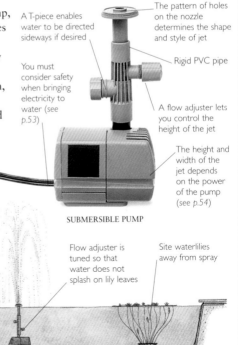

A T-piece enables water to be directed sideways if desired

The pattern of holes on the nozzle determines the shape and style of jet

Rigid PVC pipe

You must consider safety when bringing electricity to water (see p.53)

A flow adjuster lets you control the height of the jet

The height and width of the jet depends on the power of the pump (see p.54)

SUBMERSIBLE PUMP

Free-floating plants will be drawn toward the pump as it sucks in water, which can be a nuisance

Flow adjuster is tuned so that water does not splash on lily leaves

Site waterlilies away from spray

◄ USING WALLS *A wall fountain (p.46) brings sparkle to a shady corner in a small courtyard garden.*

MAKING A RIVER ROCK FOUNTAIN

Reservoir features, in which water gushes up from the ground from a sunken, concealed reservoir housing the pump, are an ideal solution where space does not permit a pool, or to add interest to rock gardens or plantings in gravel with an Oriental feel. Here, river rocks are used as the decorative covering; millstones are also popular (but fiberglass ones are easier to handle and less expensive) or, with a longer length of pipe, you can make the water spill from a bamboo ornament or urn (*see overleaf*).

▶ SELF-CONTAINED APPEAL
Beach-washed pebbles or stones look beautiful when wet, another attraction of these small, safe features.

YOU NEED:

TOOLS
- Tape measure
- Spade or shovel
- Carpenter's level
- Rake
- Wirecutters
- Tamping tool

MATERIALS
- Large plastic tub or garbage can
- 6ft×6ft/2×2m heavy polyethylene sheet
- Submersible pump with filter
- Short length of delivery pipe with flow adjuster
- Brick base for pump
- Square of galvanized metal mesh 4in/10cm wider than diameter of tub
- River rocks

DIGGING THE HOLE

1 Measure the depth and width – including handles – of the tub, then dig a hole that is slightly wider and deeper. Keep trying the tub out in the hole until the depth is right. Then use a level to make sure that the tub will be level.

2 Settle in the tub and backfill around it, poking soil down firmly with the tamping tool. Rake the surrounding area to remove stones, drawing the soil slightly away from the edges of the tub to create a saucer-shaped depression around it.

LAYING POLYETHYLENE AND INSTALLING THE PUMP

1 **Lay the polyethylene** sheet over the prepared area and cut out a circle 2in/5cm smaller in diameter than the plastic tub. The sheet collects the pumped-up water, and the dip lets it drain back into the reservoir.

2 **Connect the delivery pipe** with flow adjuster to the pump outlet (*see p.54*), but do not trim the pipe to length. Put the brick base in the bottom of the tub, then lower the pump onto it so that it acts as a plinth.

3 **Center the galvanized** mesh over the hole in the polyethylene, then use wire-cutters to cut a small hole in the middle, just wide enough for the delivery pipe, and feed the pipe up through it. You can give the cable extra protection under the stones by feeding it through rigid piping. Fill the tub with water, to about 2–3in/5–8cm from the top.

ADDING THE RIVER ROCK

1 **Arrange a few stones** around the pipe and cut it to length. Then turn the pump on and judge the effect; you will probably need to remove the stones and mesh once or twice to tweak the flow adjuster.

2 **Once the fountain effect** is right, with the pump on, arrange the rest of the river rocks. Once the area onto which the water falls is established, trim surplus polyethylene, burying the edges under the soil.

CASCADES AND CANALS

A low-voltage pump can push water for a distance of about 6½ft/2m on level ground; this grows less the more it has to travel uphill. Even so, it provides opportunity for many features: a rocky cascade on a gentle gradient, a level canal spilling into a small formal pool; an ornament, perhaps an urn, on the side of a pool from which water brims over; a wall fountain (*overleaf*), and variations on simple reservoir features such as the river rock fountain.

A BRIMMING URN

The simple principle of recirculating water demonstrated by the river rock fountain (*see previous pages*) can be expanded to include a decorative outflow for the water.

Urns and pots suit both formal and informally styled gardens, but the choice is up to you – Japanese-style bamboo ornaments such as the *shishi odoshi*, or deer-scarer, are popular, as are novelty items: old-fashioned cast-iron pumps, running faucets, or permanently watering watering cans. For a contemporary look, choose an urn or pot with a colored glaze, and complement it with pebbles of colored glass below that will glow and sparkle under the falling water.

▶ RUNAWAY SUCCESS
Restful and elegant, this brimming urn draws both the eye and the ear with a gentle splashing onto pebbles amid lush planting.

HOW IT WORKS

Make the feature exactly as for the river rock fountain on the previous pages, but use a longer length of flexible pipe and leave it untrimmed. You need an urn with a drainage hole in the base through which to feed the pipe; then seal it in with a mastic sealant or similar, letting this dry completely before filling the urn with water. Whatever container you use, it must be frostproof to survive a cold winter or brought under cover. If you are leaving it outside, you should be sure that it is empty: if water freezes solid, it will crack the pot. Check that nothing has taken up residence in it in the spring!

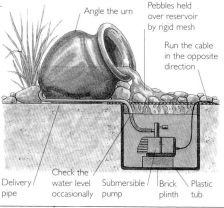

Angle the urn

Pebbles held over reservoir by rigid mesh

Run the cable in the opposite direction

Delivery pipe

Check the water level occasionally

Submersible pump

Brick plinth

Plastic tub

A SIMPLE WATERCOURSE

You can extend your pool or pond's appeal by adding a short watercourse with a concealed outlet or header pool. A formal canal (*right and below*) usually suits a regular pool, particularly one surrounded by hard landscaping, while a tumbling, slightly meandering rocky cascade (*as shown on pp.14 and 55*) often looks good with an informal feature. For the latter, you can set or mortar loose rocks over flexible liner (as for the slabs below), or buy rigid, preformed plastic or fiberglass stone-effect cascade units.

The gradient of the watercourse can be so shallow as to be virtually invisible, or you can make a shorter, steeper slope, on which it is advisable to place rocks randomly to interrupt the water. On a smooth slope, water tends to look as if it is being tipped down, rather than flowing naturally. The rocks will break up the flow, creating splashing and movement, appropriate to a mountainside rivulet.

INTEGRATING THE FEATURE
This small canal lifts the interest of the regular pool. The materials used blend in well with the pool edging and the landscaped edges.

HOW IT WORKS

A canal leading out from one side can be added to an existing pool, whether it has a rigid or flexible liner. Make sure that the strip of liner you use to line the trench is wide enough to cover the sides and edges, and has a good flap of overlap to press down over the pool's side. Chunky gravel or pebbles that will not be swept along could be used without mortar on the canal floor instead of slabs.

Facing bricks disguise the liner — Water channel — Slab

CROSS SECTION

BUILDING THE CANAL
A shallow trench leading to the pool, sloping fractionally downward, is lined with a strip of butyl, hidden by decorative slabs and side walls (above right).

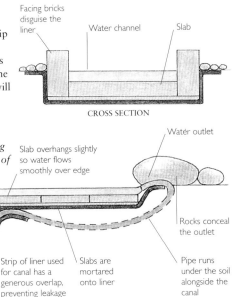

Water outlet

Slab overhangs slightly so water flows smoothly over edge

Rocks conceal the outlet

T-piece with vertical outlet capped

Submersible pump

Strip of liner used for canal has a generous overlap, preventing leakage

Slabs are mortared onto liner

Pipe runs under the soil alongside the canal

MOUNTING A WALL FOUNTAIN

Wall fountains bring water to patios, courtyards, and enclosed gardens; they are ideal where there is insufficient space for a full-scale pool. Antique stone masks are expensive, but new, textured plaster and fiberglass versions are convincing and, being lighter, can be attached easily onto a trellis. The reservoir can be open and planted, as here, or covered over and concealed.

YOU NEED:

TOOLS
- Pencil, awl • Drill
- Screwdriver

MATERIALS
- 6½ft×24in/ 2m×60cm trellis panel
- Two 24in/60cm wooden slats
- Screws, anchors
- Lightweight mask with 6½ft/2m delivery piping and right-angled outlet pipe
- Small submersible pump
- Trough or tub as reservoir

ATTACHING THE TRELLIS

1 **Hold the trellis** against the wall (it should not rest on bare earth) and mark the position of the top and base on the wall. Make sure the trellis runs parallel to lines of brickwork.

2 **Drill 3 equally spaced** holes along one slat and hold it against the top mark. Make guide marks on the brick, then drill holes (*inset*).

3 **Insert anchors** (*inset*) into the holes, then screw the slat onto the wall. Repeat Steps 2 and 3 with the lower slat.

4 **Screw the trellis panel** to the slats. Holding the panel firmly (get some help if you need it), with the vertical struts nearest the wall (this is important), drill holes through the struts and into the top slat, then insert screws and tighten them (*see inset*). Repeat at the base of the panel.

ATTACHING THE FOUNTAIN MASK

1 **Hold the mask** where you want it (just below eye level often looks best), and mark through the holes onto a horizontal strut.

2 **With the trellis** facing this way, the delivery pipe can be threaded up behind the horizontal struts to approximately the right level.

3 **The rigid right-angle** outlet connector prevents kinks in the pipe as it turns to be threaded through the mask's mouth.

4 **Screw the mask** to the horizontal trellis strut. If the mask does not have holes (most of the lightweight cast or molded ones do), you can use a couple of mirror plates.

5 **Connect the pipe** to the outlet of the pump, and stand the pump on a brick in the reservoir. Fill the reservoir, turn on the pump, and adjust the flow as desired.

FINISHED FEATURE
Planting in and around the reservoir hides the pump, while climbing plants cover the trellis and disguise the vertical delivery pipe.

PLANNING AND PLANT CARE

SITING AND STOCKING

WHILE YOU HAVE A LOT OF FREEDOM in choosing the design and style of your water feature, siting needs careful thought and may be restricted by a number of factors: availability of light, and the position of underground utilities (*see overleaf*), for example. While wildlife appreciates a secluded pond, a good, clear view from the house or patio is essential in a family garden.

SUN AND SHELTER FOR A PLANTED POND

Water plants need plenty of sun, but ponds, especially informal ones, can look out of place in exposed sites. Shelter is advisable, but before you position a pond by a boundary or densely planted area, check that it will not be shaded (*below*), and consider bringing it more into the open, particularly if the water will then reflect the sky – a lovely effect.

SITING TIPS

• Avoid cold, windy sites, frost pockets, and also sun traps, where water will evaporate.
• Don't site a pond under a tree or large shrub; falling leaves will pollute the water.
• Make sure there is easy access to the pond and to plantings beyond it.
• Sloping sites can cause extra work.

Avoid deep shade

Dappled or part-day shade can be acceptable, provided that branches do not overhang open water

A pond in this sunny area could be viewed from the house

◄ MAPPING SHADE
Plot the changing areas of sunlight and shade through the day before choosing a site.

▼ REFLECTIVE POTENTIAL
Lay a mirror on the ground to see what will be reflected in the water.

KEY TO DAILY SHADE PATTERN

	EARLY MORNING		NOON		EARLY EVENING

◄ CLEAR WATER *Choosing an advantageous position is essential to healthy plant growth.*

OTHER SITING PRACTICALITIES

Never start to dig a hole unless you know you are not going to hit underground pipes or cabling. When you bought your property, you probably learned where these crossed your garden, but if not, consult your local utility companies. You also should not obstruct manhole covers and other inspection facilities such as water meters, or undermine or damage neighboring structures such as walls and fences.

Remember that the nearer your water feature is to the house, the easier it will be to run electricity to it to power a pump or lighting. If building a garden from scratch, laying plastic pipes as future cable conduits under any paving will be a great boon.

▶ PROCESS OF ELIMINATION
In an average small back garden, the ideal position for a pond may present itself through a combination of factors, both practical and aesthetic.

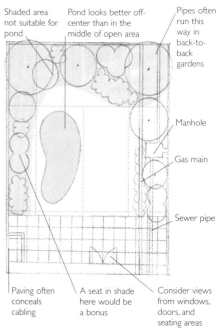

Shaded area not suitable for pond

Pond looks better off-center than in the middle of open area

Pipes often run this way in back-to-back gardens

Manhole

Gas main

Sewer pipe

Paving often conceals cabling

A seat in shade here would be a bonus

Consider views from windows, doors, and seating areas

SIZES AND SHAPES

Big pools and ponds entail more work but give much more opportunity for plantings. A pond is easier to keep healthy with a minimum surface area of about 40sq ft/ 4sq m, in which a good balance of functional plants (*see facing page*) for the volume of water can be achieved. A depth of at least 20in/50cm is essential (or marginal areas of 12in/30cm with a deep zone of about 3ft/1m); otherwise evaporation, and in cold climates, freezing water, will be a problem. Keep shapes simple for ease of construction.

SIMPLE SHAPES
It is tempting to complicate the edges of a lined pool for interest, but you will find it much easier to build a very simple curved shape, then place or mortar rocks on top of the liner to create promontories and inlets. You also have the advantage of being able to vary the effect.

FUNCTIONAL PLANTS FOR HEALTHY WATER

A pool of any size with no plants needs a filter to keep the water clear, but plants do the job very efficiently if the right ones are chosen, and in the right quantities. You *must* include two categories of plants – submerged weeds to oxygenate the water, and floating-leaved plants to cover about one-third to half of the surface, which provide some shelter from the sun. These two plant types will help minimize the inevitable algal growth in all ponds. See *Plants for Water Features (pp.63–77)*.

GETTING IT RIGHT

SUBMERGED PLANTS

Too few
Without enough plants below the surface to keep the water well oxygenated and to compete with the tiny plants known as algae, these quickly multiply and take over to "green" the water.

MYRIOPHYLLUM AQUATICUM

Too many
The pond becomes completely clogged with growth, and other functional and decorative plants have difficulty thriving. If floating-leaved plants succumb, algae will multiply.

FLOATING PLANTS

Too few
Sunlight encourages the rapid growth of algae in the water, depleting it of oxygen and preventing the natural processing of debris by aquatic creatures: the pond becomes clogged and foul.

NYMPHAEA

Too many
Plants below the surface, shaded of all light, die and decompose: the rotting plant material releases methane gas, which is trapped in the water, upsetting the balance of aquatic life. The water may become black and smelly, and other plants die.

ADDING MORE TO THE POND

Once you have a good balance of submerged and floating-leaved plants in a pond (any good supplier will be able to advise on quantities of plants to buy), you may add as many, or as few, marginal and poolside plants as you desire: these are purely decorative additions that have no effect on the health of the water. You may, for aesthetic reasons, prefer to stock lightly; or, with conservation issues in mind, design well-planted margins so that wildlife feels secure in approaching and using the pond. Fish-keeping is beyond the scope of this book, save only to say that healthy water (*see above*) is absolutely essential for them.

◄ EDGING EXTRAS
The range of marginal and moisture-loving plants, like this Houttuynia, that you can add is varied (see pp.70–77).

▶ FIRST FISH
Easy, hardy fish for beginners include the ubiquitous goldfish, many comets, and shubunkin.

WATER AND SAFETY

ALWAYS CONSIDER SAFETY when planning a water feature, especially if the garden is used by young children or the less mobile and sure-footed, or domestic animals. There are a number of materials with textured surfaces to use as non-slip edging, for example. Water and electricity do not mix, so you must take extra precautions if you want to bring power to your water feature.

SAFETY FOR CHILDREN

Many people opt not to have water in the garden at all when children are young; converting a pond excavation into a sandbox for the duration is a popular choice. But you can make ponds safe with mesh (below), provided that children are supervised around them. A mini-pool, container garden, or a small pond with a beach are all reasonably safe and fascinating for older children. Or, choose a feature that has no open surface of water, such as a bubble fountain (see below and p.42).

(see below and p.42)

► MESH BARRIER
Use bricks to support heavy-duty rigid wire mesh just below the water surface. Make sure that the mesh fits the pond exactly so that it is stable.

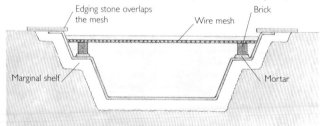

Edging stone overlaps the mesh | Brick | Wire mesh | Marginal shelf | Mortar

◄PATIO FEATURES
The movement, sound, and convenient height of a brimming urn are irresistible to a small child. Make it safe by setting it over a covered reservoir and filling the urn up with pebbles. Taking the pebbles out may suggest itself as a good game, however, so watch over children as they play.

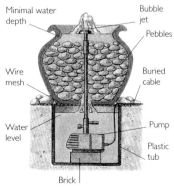

Minimal water depth | Bubble jet | Pebbles | Wire mesh | Buried cable | Water level | Pump | Plastic tub | Brick

BRINGING ELECTRICITY TO THE GARDEN

Electricity outdoors can be a hazard: all cabling and connectors must be waterproof and specifically sold for outdoor use. Extra low-voltage equipment, suitable for most small features, is by far the easiest and safest choice; with it, a transformer within the house converts the power supply to a very low and safe one, minimizing danger. Larger cascades and fountains must have a circuit-breaker and ground fault interrupter (GFI).

POWER TIPS

• Always follow the manufacturer's instructions.

• If in any doubt, employ a qualified electrician to set up your electrical system: it is well worth the investment for peace of mind.

• Use only switches, cable, and connectors that are clearly safety-approved for outdoor use.

• Switch off and disconnect equipment before handling.

• Don't position connectors under water.

• If absent-minded, consider fitting a timer to turn the feature off at night.

• Wrap and tape plastic securely over the ends of connectors if removing the pump for winter storage or servicing.

EXTRA LOW VOLTAGE SYSTEM
Extra low-voltage equipment is used in conjunction with a transformer and presents no danger from shock. The transformer must be placed indoors and as close to the wall socket as possible.

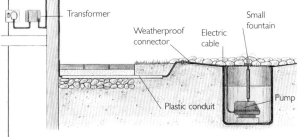

Transformer
Weatherproof connector
Electric cable
Small fountain
Pump
Plastic conduit

LIGHTING WATER FEATURES

Carefully positioned lighting brings a new beauty to water and plants, as well as extending the hours of viewing. A safe, extra low-voltage system (*as above*) is powerful enough to light a group of plants or a small pool with a small fountain (combined pumps and lights are available in kit form). If you already have a pump or outdoor lighting and are considering adding pond lighting using the existing power supply, consult your supplier or a qualified electrician for advice on its capacity.

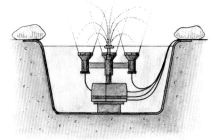

FOUNTAIN AND LIGHTING KIT
Three regularly spaced lights around the nozzle provide even uplighting for the spray – impossible to achieve with a single lamp.

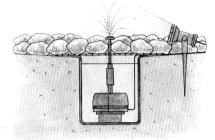

SURFACE LIGHTING
An angled spotlight made for outdoor use will illuminate small, bubbling fountains. Hide the casing among plants or stones.

USING PUMPS WITH WATER FEATURES

ALTHOUGH SOLAR-POWERED PUMPS are becoming more widely available, the most popular choice in domestic gardens is still the small, electrically powered submersible pump. Neat and quiet, easy to install, and with their own integral filters, these modern pumps bear no resemblance to the infernal machines of the past, and using extra low-voltage power (*see previous page*) are very safe.

CHOOSING THE RIGHT PUMP

Pumps come in a wide range of sizes to suit every type of water feature. An extra low-voltage submersible pump will send water either upward or sideways for a distance of around 4ft/1.2m, which is adequate for most small features. A water garden specialist or a nursery with a good aquatic department stocking pumps will be more than happy to advise on the capacity of pump you need for the feature you have in mind; many manufacturers also have telephone help lines. It helps them to know what size your water feature is (multiply the surface area by the average depth for approximate volume of water), how far the water will travel, and what you hope the effect will be.

SUBMERSIBLE PUMPS
These self-contained, submersible pumps are suitable for a range of small fountains and watercourses.

HOW IT WORKS

Small submersible pumps suck water in through a filter, to keep out debris, then propel it either upward or, via a T-piece, sideways along a pipe. Plastic delivery pipes usually come separately, to be bought by length in a range of widths. Other fountain nozzles are available, with varied spray, jet, and bubble effects: the last of these allows the least evaporation. Once the pump is installed and running, you can use the flow adjuster to vary the rate at which water is pumped.

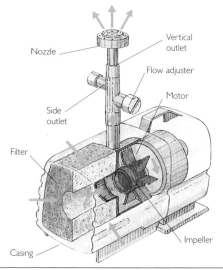

Nozzle

Vertical outlet

Flow adjuster

Motor

Side outlet

Filter

Casing

Impeller

PRACTICAL TIPS

• Choose a known brand for service support, and make sure all accessories are present.
• Overestimate the length of pipe you need.
• Never allow the pump to run dry; this will damage the motor.

MAKING MOVING WATER LOOK NATURAL

For the fastest or strongest flow, let the water take the shortest route between pump and outlet. The farther the water has to travel through a pipe, the more it will be slowed down by friction. When sending water out of the pool to the head of a canal or watercourse, hide the pump under an overhang or behind rocks at the side of the pool, making sure that the electric cable will reach dry land, to avoid the need to connect cables underwater. A central fountain in an open pool presents the most problems in concealing the pump. You can either set up a remote arrangement, whereby the pump is at the side of the pool and a flexible pipe takes the water to a nozzle on a stand in the center, or choose a fountain ornament (*below*). Pipes or cables crossing the pool floor may be concealed with gravel. Never settle a pump into mud on the pool floor to hide it: pumps should always be placed on a plinth (a brick will do) to reduce the amount of bottom sludge sucked into the strainer.

CASCADING WATERCOURSE
A natural look is achieved with randomly placed rocks and informal planting. The way the water falls over the "spill stone" is crucial; you can check this (inset) *as you position it.*

FOUNTAIN ORNAMENTS

Pool ornaments that incorporate fountains and cascades of water come in a large range of styles, although the "classical" look still wins hands down in the popularity stakes. Be aware that many of the ornaments on display at craft fairs are suitable only for indoor or conservatory use. With most, a delivery pipe is fed in from a pump at the side of the pool, or a short length of pipe is run up from the fountain outlet of a pump hidden below the ornament within an integral plinth.

▲ PLINTH FOR A PUMP
This cherub fountain ornament (right) *is typical in having a hollow plinth that is placed over a small submersible pump to disguise it.*

▶ FINISHING THE FEATURE
The pipe is then fed up through the ornament to its spout, where there will be a press-on or, occasionally, a screw attachment for the pipe; if the latter, a simple hose attachment will be required for the end of the delivery pipe.

PLANTING A POND

O<small>NE OF THE MAJOR EXCITEMENTS</small> of creating water features is the opportunity to shop for and plant a whole new range of plants. Water plants are very easy to grow successfully; given a sunny site (*see p.49*), well-balanced stocking (*see p.51*), and the maintenance of healthy pond conditions, they will start to look established by the end of their first growing season.

SELECTING PLANTS, CONTAINERS, AND SOIL

Midspring is the best time of year to buy plants, with mild weather making it easier for them to establish and plenty of time to grow. Provide enough functional plants (*see p.51*) right from the start. Waterlilies may well be your floating-leaved plants of choice, but they take time to cover the surface adequately. It is worth buying some faster-growing free-floating plants at first, such as *Azolla filiculoides* (*see pp.63–65*), even if these are only temporary.

You *must not* use ordinary potting soils; they are too rich, and their nutrients leach into the water to feed algae. Most aquatic nurseries will have special aquatic soil mix, which is ideal; in a pinch, ordinary, unfed garden soil can be used.

WATER PLANTS ON DISPLAY
From midspring to midsummer, plenty of plants will be on display. Choose healthy, compact young specimens with fresh growth.

PLANTING BASKETS
These open-sided aquatic containers are recommended for small ponds. They make plants very manageable, restraining their spread and making lifting and dividing easy.

Make sure there is enough overlap to prevent soil from escaping

USING LINING
Always line large-meshed containers to keep the soil in. Burlap is an ideal material, allowing gases and water through while preventing the soil from escaping.

SUBMERGED AND FLOATING PLANTS

Bunches (*right*) of submerged oxygenating plants are usually dropped directly into large informal ponds, where they tend to root in bottom sludge, then spread without restriction. However, in smaller ponds it is better to plant them in containers (*see below*) so that you can control their growth. A 12in/30cm crate will accommodate several bunches. If you are planting more than one species, keep each type to a separate container.

With free-floating plants, such as *Azolla filiculoides* and *Stratiotes aloides*, simply place them onto the surface of the pond.

1 **Line a container** with burlap and fill with damp soil. Make holes about 2in/5cm deep and insert the bunches of oxygenating plants (here *Lagarosiphon major*).

2 **Firm in the plants** with your fingers and trim off any excess lining. Topdress with gravel to stop the soil from floating off, and lower the basket gently into the pond.

PLANTING BARE-ROOT DEEP-WATER PLANTS

Most water plants that are sold bare-root, such as waterlilies, have swollen, fleshy roots (tubers or rhizomes) which must not be allowed to dry out. It should be obvious which ones should be planted horizontally and which vertically; if not, ask. They should be positioned fairly near the soil surface. Depending on the depth of your pond, the plant may need a temporary stack of bricks under its basket so that its young shoots just reach the surface. Remove the bricks gradually as the plant grows.

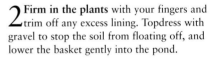

Trim back long, coarse roots

1 **Use pruners to** remove roots that are damaged or excessively long. Then cut off any large, old, or completely unfurled leaves at the base.

2 **Line the basket** and fill nearly to the top with dampened soil. Position the tuber or rhizome within 1½in/4cm of the rim.

3 **Add more soil** and firm, taking care not to damage new shoots. Topdress with gravel so that soil does not float off and expose the root.

STABILIZING MARGINAL PLANTS

Marginals grow well in planting baskets (*see previous page*), which can be positioned in natural-looking groups. Another advantage is that you can move the plants around until you are satisfied with the effect and lift them easily for dividing and thinning. With most of their growth above water, tall marginal plants such as irises can become top-heavy, and you may need to stabilize them (*below*).

USING A BRICK
If using a planting basket to house a tall marginal, place a brick in the bottom of the container before adding damp soil. The weight will firmly anchor the basket.

USING A THICK TOPDRESSING
Alternatively, to allow more space for roots to grow, use a thick layer of pea gravel or pebbles on top of the soil. This also provides a decorative finish.

PLANTING MOISTURE-LOVING PLANTS

Planting directly into permanently moist soil at the edges of a pond or in a bog garden is no different from planting in a border, as long as you are careful not to compact the soil too much. However, be sure not to add fertilizer or manure to any area of soil from which it might leach into the water, feeding algae and disrupting the pond's environmental balance. Remember that moisture-loving plants grow very vigorously in the damp soil they enjoy, so it is important to allow them plenty of room.

1 **Dig a hole in the** soil large enough to accommodate the roots and accompanying soil. Support the plant (here *Caltha palustris*), and gently ease it out of the container.

2 **Place the plant in** the hole at the same depth as it was in the container. Use your hands to firm the soil around the crown (where root and stem join). Water thoroughly.

POND AND PLANT MAINTENANCE

PROVIDED THAT YOU HAVE DONE ALL the necessary preparation well – good planning, construction, and stocking – it should not be difficult to tend your pond. Thinning and dividing of plants will be necessary, probably from the third year on; emptying and cleaning is an infrequently needed operation.

THINNING PLANTS IN THE WATER

Submerged plants or pond weeds usually multiply rapidly and may need thinning once or twice in the growing season. You may also need to skim off free-floating plants, particularly if more decorative floating-leaved plants are maturing and providing the necessary surface cover. Most pond weeds can take any amount of damage; do not worry about tearing stems off. If you notice a type of filamentous underwater plant growth like wet, green cotton, it is blanketweed, a form of algae, and should be removed: twirl a stick around in it like spaghetti to lift it out.

CONTROLLING RAMPANT GROWTH
Thin out overgrown pond weed and small floating plants with a fishing net or by "combing" the water with a rake.

DIVIDING MARGINALS AND MOISTURE-LOVERS

Plants that are overwhelming others or have crowded growth (planting baskets often accentuate this), possibly flowering less freely, need to be divided. Many moisture-loving and marginal plants (see *Plants for Water Features* for specific advice) form clumps of fibrous roots that are easily pulled apart with your hands and divided into smaller sections. Irises can look a little more tricky; their knotty clusters of fleshy rhizomes must be cut into portions, each with some shoot growth (*below*).

1 **Lift the iris** (here *Iris pseudacorus*) and rinse soil off the roots. You can split apart large masses of fleshy rhizomes with your hands; if necessary, use a knife.

2 **Use a sharp garden knife** to trim the rhizome neatly, removing any portions that do not show any new growth shoots. Trim the roots and leaves back to 3–4in/6–10cm.

3 **Replant carefully, filling** in fresh soil around the rhizome, so that the roots are not compressed. Topdress with pea gravel and reposition in the pond.

DIVIDING WATERLILIES

A waterlily in need of dividing has crowded leaves that start to thrust out of the water, rather than lying flat. It may be flowering less freely, too. It should be lifted and split (*below*); if you have a large pond, replant several portions in separate baskets and place them around the pond. Waterlilies enjoy an annual feeding, especially when newly divided, but do not add ordinary garden fertilizers, which will wash out into the water. You can buy suitable coated, slow-release aquatic fertilizer from garden centers to push into the soil.

► CROWDED GROWTH
The lifted waterlily will have a mass of stems and leaves, a response to having exhausted the soil nutrients. Ease it from its planting basket to divide the roots.

Strong new shoots

Top-dressing of gravel

1 **Carefully lift the plant** and rinse off the soil. Remove all opened leaves, and cut the rhizome in two, retaining the part with the most vigorous young emerging roots.

2 **Trim long, coarse roots,** replant with the crown just below soil level, and reposition the waterlily in the pond on a stack of bricks (*see p.33*). Discard the old portion of rhizome.

REMOVING DEAD LEAVES

Decaying leaves turn pond water into a nutritious soup for algae, so try and remove as many as possible. Snip off dying and dead leaves from water plants, and remove them whenever possible.
In autumn, to prevent leaves from blowing into the pool, netting is helpful. Trim herbaceous poolside plants back in autumn so that debris does not detach and drift into the pond.

CUTTING OFF DEAD LEAVES
Trimming dying or damaged leaves back with a sharp knife keeps pond and plants healthy.

NETTING IN AUTUMN
Anchor plastic netting across the pond with bricks to trap autumn leaves.

WINTER PRECAUTIONS

In areas where winter means snow and ice, ponds must be deep enough (*see p.32*) not to freeze solid. Move any exposed container plants under cover. Most water plants will die back and lie dormant, but the pond must still have air, which a sheet of surface ice will seal off. The pressure exerted by ice can easily fracture a rigid liner. A pressure-absorbing float, such as a ball or piece of wood, will absorb some of the stress as the pond freezes, but a stock tank deicer is the most effective protection.

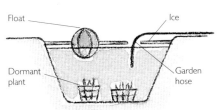

ABSORBING PRESSURE
Compressible floats such as a rubber ball will absorb the pressure of expanding water as it freezes. You can siphon some water out to create a dead-air space beneath the ice.

EMPTYING A POND

A pond's environmental balance takes years to establish, and all of its inhabitants will resent it being disrupted by over-frequent emptying and refilling. However, every four or five years your pond may need an overhaul – or, in a lined pond, you may suspect a leak is responsible for falling water levels, and repairing it (*below*) involves emptying the pool. Protect all of the plants: wrap plants in baskets in wet newspaper, and keep floating plants and submerged plants in a bucket of water. Try to empty and refill in one day unless you need to repair a leak in the liner. If the pond has a pump, it can be used to pump water out; if not, it must be siphoned off to expose the sludge.

1 **When the pond** is empty of water, mud can be scooped up carefully with a small plastic spade or a dustpan (never use sharp metal tools). You may need to brush or wipe down the whole liner to find a leak.

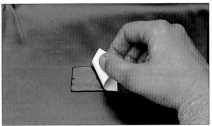

2 **Let the damaged area dry**, and clean with a cloth and a little alcohol. Place double-sided adhesive tape over the puncture.

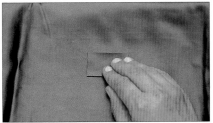

3 **Cut a patch from** a spare piece of liner and press firmly onto the tape, making sure that the edges are flat.

PLANTS FOR WATER FEATURES

This catalog includes a wide range of popular water plants, especially those suited to small ponds. The plants have been grouped according to their planting environments. Throughout the catalog, maximum planting depths and plant dimensions are given, while symbols provide a quick reference to growing needs.

Submerged plant *Floating-leaved plant* *Free-floating plant* *Waterlily* *Lotus*
Marginal plant *Prefers full sun* *Prefers partial shade* *Tolerates shade*
Prefers well-drained but moisture-retentive soil *Prefers moist soil* *Prefers wet soil*
Hardiness zone ranges are given as **Zx–xx** *or* *Tender*

DEEP-WATER AND FLOATING PLANTS

THESE PLANTS ARE VITAL to keep pond water healthy. Submerged leaves raise oxygen levels, while floating leaves provide shade. Submerged plants may grow completely underwater or have leafy growth both above and below the surface; others float freely. There are also alternatives to waterlilies (*see p.66*): plants that need their roots in deep water, while their leaves float on the surface.

Aponogeton distachyos (Cape pondweed, water hawthorn) A less showy alternative to waterlilies for an informal or wildlife pond, this deep-water perennial may be almost evergreen in mild winters. It produces heavily scented white flowers in forked clusters, either in two flushes or throughout summer. Divide the fleshy roots in spring. Depth to 2ft/60cm; spread 4ft/1.2m. **Z9–10**

Azolla filiculoides (syn. *A. caroliniana*) (Fairy moss) Tiny, free-floating perennial fern that multiplies to form

CERATOPHYLLUM DEMERSUM

clusters of soft, pale green leaves, each with a single fine root, that turn purplish red in autumn. Useful for rapid,

temporary cover in a new pond while other plants grow. Thin regularly in summer. May quickly become invasive. Any depth; spread indefinite. **Z7–11**

Ceratophyllum demersum (Hornwort) Deciduous, underwater perennial, with slender stems and feathery leaves. Shade-tolerant, it will grow in deeper water than many oxygenators. Young plantlets form and break away, or can be detached, from the parent. May need thinning in a small pond. Depth to 2ft/60cm; spread indefinite. **Z6–9**

◀ *TRAPA NATANS This unusual floating plant (see p.65) bears shiny black fruits after hot summers.*

HOTTONIA PALUSTRIS

HYDROCHARIS MORSUS-RANAE

Hottonia palustris
(Water violet)
Deciduous, oxygenating perennial that can also be used as a marginal plant, forming spreading masses of light green, deeply divided foliage held both below and above the water surface. White, mauve, or pale lilac flower spikes emerge above the water in spring. Best added to an established pond with well-balanced water chemistry. Thin periodically. Depth to 18in/45cm, spread indefinite. ▣ ▣ **Z5–11**

Hydrocharis morsus-ranae
(Frogbit)
Perennial free-floating plant with rosettes of kidney-shaped, shiny leaves and papery white flowers with a yellow center. The female flowers are borne singly, the male ones in clusters of 3–4. Excellent surface cover for a wildlife pond, it prefers still, shallow water (it may root in muddy marginal zones) and provides useful shelter for aquatic creatures, although it is vulnerable to snail damage.

New plantlets form on spreading stems. Rooting depth to 12in/30cm, spread indefinite.
▣ ▣ **Z6–11**

Lagarosiphon major
(syn. *Elodea crispa*)
Oxygenating plant forming dense, underwater masses of branching, fragile stems covered in narrow, curving leaves. Tiny, translucent flower heads develop in summer. Thin in summer and cut back dying growth in autumn. Depth to 3ft/1m, spread indefinite. ▣ ▣ **Z8–11**

Marsilea quadrifolia
(Water clover)
Scrambling perennial with long, creeping roots. It is a fern but has shamrocklike leaves, downy when young; they float flat on the surface or may stand above the water in shallows. Divide in spring. Depth to 2ft/60cm, spread indefinite. ▣ ▣ **Z6–11**

Myriophyllum
Perennial oxygenators with spreading stems and tightly packed, delicate, bright green leaves, ideal for shallow water, where the feathery stems extend above the surface, bearing spikes of inconspicuous, yellowish flowers. *M. verticillatum* (milfoil) is very hardy (Z3–11), but *M. aquaticum* (parrot feather, Z9–11) will not survive cold winters. Depth to 18in/45cm, spread indefinite. ▣ ▣ Hardiness varies

Nuphar (Yellow pond lilies)
Deciduous deep-water perennials with large, floating leaves and round, yellow flowers with chunky bosses of red-tinted stamens, held just

NYMPHOIDES PELTATA

NUPHAR JAPONICA

above the surface in summer. Unlike waterlilies, they tolerate moving water. *Nuphar lutea* (Z6–11) has the largest flowers, but some people dislike the smell. *N. japonica* (Z6–9), the Japanese pond lily, is similar but needs hot summers to flower freely; *N. advena* (Z3–10) or *N. pumila* (Z4–8) are better choices for colder areas. Divide in spring. Depth to 12in/30cm, spread 3ft/1m. ▨ ☑ Hardiness varies

Nymphoides peltata
(Fringed waterlily, water fringe, yellow floating heart) Deciduous perennial with floating, mid-green leaves, often splashed with brown. Throughout summer, small, golden yellow flowers with fringed petals are held just above the water surface. Divide the rhizomatous roots in spring. Depth 6–18in/15–45cm, spread 2ft/60cm. ▨ ☑ **Z6–11**

Pistia stratiotes
(Water lettuce, shell flower) Deciduous, tender, free-floating plant, evergreen in tropical waters or in a heated conservatory. Overlapping, velvety, pale green leaves, whitish green on the underside, are clustered like a lettuce. Produces tiny greenish flowers. Thin or detach new plantlets in summer. Spread indefinite.
▨ ☑ ◈

Potamogeton crispus
(Curled pondweed) Oxygenating plant with seaweedlike submerged leaves holding crimson and creamy white flowers just above the water in summer. Spreads rapidly in bottom silt and tolerates cloudy or shaded water well. Depth to 3ft/1m, spread indefinite.
▨ ☑ **Z7–11**

Salvinia auriculata
Free-floating fern forming spreading colonies. The pale green or purplish brown leaves are covered in silky hairs and tightly packed on branched stems. Remove faded foliage regularly and thin or detach young plantlets in summer. Spread indefinite.
▨ ☑ **Z10–11**

PISTIA STRATIOTES

SALVINIA AURICULATA

Stratiotes aloides
(Water soldier) Semi-evergreen, free-floating perennial forming "pineapple-top" rosettes of spiky leaves held partly below and partly above water. Plantlets form on spreading stems: detach in summer as new plants, or thin at any time. Spread indefinite.
▨ ☑ **Z5–11**

Trapa natans
(Water chestnut) Floating annual forming rosettes of diamond-shaped, brown-patterned leaves (*see p.62*). White flowers are followed by shiny, spiny, angular black fruits. Spread indefinite. ▨ ☑

Utricularia vulgaris
(Greater bladderwort) Deciduous free-floating perennial with feathery, bronze-green, bladderlike leaves that trap insects. Pouched yellow flowers, with red-brown streaks, are held above the water in summer. Detach young plantlets in spring or summer. Depth to 3ft/1m, spread 2–3ft/ 60cm–1m. ▨ ☑ **Z5–9**

WATERLILIES

THE RANGE OF WATERLILIES (*Nymphaea*) is ever increasing, with new varieties continually being developed. Their exquisite flowers are often delicately perfumed, and some change color as they open. There are waterlilies for most climates and size and depth of pond, although all need sun, shelter, and still, or nearly still, water. Tropical waterlilies (Z10–11) may be grown as annuals in colder areas. Waterlilies stop flowering when overgrown.

Nymphaea 'Blue Beauty'
Free-flowering, with unusual coloring; brown-flecked wavy-edged leaves, with purplish undersides. Scented, semidouble flowers have rich blue petals and yellow stamens. In cool areas, plant out in late spring; overwinter under glass. Depth 12–24in/30–60cm, spread 4–6ft/1.2–2m. ✿ ❀ Z10–11

Nymphaea capensis
(Cape blue waterlily)
Tender, for warm areas or a large container pond under cover. Wavy-edged leaves up to 16in/40cm across. Semidouble, star-shaped flowers, up to 10in/25cm across, are light blue with yellow stamens. Depth 12–24in/30–60cm, spread 5–8ft/1.5–2.5m. ✿ ❀ Z10–11

NYMPHAEA 'CAROLINIANA NIVEA'

Nymphaea 'Caroliniana Nivea'
For larger ponds, at its best when planted in a large crate or basket that allows a substantial root system to develop. Leaves are almost round; the flowers semidouble, star- to cup-shaped, fragrant, ivory-white, with yellow stamens. Depth 12–24in/30–60cm, spread 4–5ft/1.2–1.5m. ✿ ❀ Z4–11

Nymphaea 'Escarboucle'
Ideal for most ponds in cool climates; stays open later than most red-flowered types. Brown-tinged young leaves mature to deep green; the semidouble flowers are crimson with golden stamens, their outer petals tipped white. Depth 12–24in/30–60cm, spread 4–5ft/1.2–1.5m. ✿ ❀ Z4–11

Nymphaea 'Froebelii'
A good choice for shallow water, ideal for barrels or small ponds. Bronzed young

NYMPHAEA 'BLUE BEAUTY'

NYMPHAEA CAPENSIS

Nymphaea 'Laydekeri Fulgens'

bright yellow stamens. Depth 18–24in/45–60cm, spread 5–8ft/1.5–2.5m. ▨ ▩ **Z10–11**

Nymphaea × *helvola* (syn. **N. 'Pygmaea Helvola'**)
Ideal for a small shallow pool or container pond. The oval, mottled purple leaves have purple undersides; the small, semidouble flowers are a clear buttercup yellow. Depth 6–8in/15–22cm, spread 2ft/60cm. ▨ ▩ **Z4–11**

Nymphaea **'James Brydon'**
A pinkish red waterlily, good for small ponds or half-barrels. Its leaves, purplish brown when young, mature to plain dark green. Double flowers, a rich rose-red, can be 5in/12cm across. Depth 12–18in/30–45cm, spread 3–4ft/1–1.2m. ▨ ▩ **Z10–11**

Nymphaea **'Laydekeri Fulgens'**
One of the first waterlilies to flower in spring, blooming freely through summer, and suitable for any size of pond. The young leaves are blotched with purple, maturing to plain green. Semidouble,

Nymphaea 'James Brydon'

burgundy-red flowers have orange-red stamens. Depth 12–18in/30–45cm, spread 4–5ft/1.2–1.5m. ▨ ▩ **Z4–11**

Nymphaea **'Marliacea Chromatella'**
One of the most reliable yellow waterlilies for any size of pond. Its coppery young leaves, with purple streaks, mature to an attractive purple-mottled mid-green. Semidouble, primrose-yellow flowers, 6in/15cm in diameter, are borne in abundance. Depth 12–18in/30–45cm, spread 4–5ft/1.2–1.5m. ▨ ▩ **Z4–11**

leaves mature to small, round or heart-shaped, pale green pads. Deep red flowers, 4–5in/10–12cm across, are first cup-shaped, then star-shaped, with orange-red stamens. Depth 6–12in/15–30cm, spread 3ft/1m. ▨▩ **Z4–11**

Nymphaea **'Gladstoneana'**
Vigorous and free-flowering; will grow large unless divided regularly. The bronzed young leaves mature to rounded, dark green pads, with crimped edges. Flowers are deep red, semidouble, star-shaped, waxy-petaled, with

Nymphaea × *helvola*

Nymphaea 'Marliacea Chromatella'

Nymphaea 'Rose Arey'

Nymphaea 'Odorata Sulphurea Grandiflora'
Bears yellow flowers that tend to open only from the late morning to early afternoon, but they are reliably produced throughout summer. Its dark green leaves are speckled with maroon; the semidouble flowers are sweetly scented, with yellow stamens. Depth 12–18in/30–45cm, spread 4–5ft/1.2–1.5cm. ⬛ 🔲 Z4–11

Nymphaea 'Robinsoniana'
Free-flowering, with attractively contrasting flowers and foliage. Its light purple

Nymphaea 'Sunrise'

leaves have deep purple blotches and red undersides. Star-shaped flowers with cupped centers, 4–5in/10–12cm across, have orange-red petals and orange stamens. Depth 12–18in/30–45cm, spread 4–5ft/1.2–1.5m. ⬛ 🔲 Z4–11

Nymphaea 'Rose Arey'
Best given a large planting container that will allow a substantial root system to develop. Purple young leaves mature to green; the anise-scented, semidouble flowers open deep pink, orange-pink at the edges, paling with age, with golden stamens. Depth 12–24in/30–60cm, spread 4–5ft/1.2–1.5m. ⬛ 🔲 Z4–11

Nymphaea 'Sunrise'
This yellow-flowered waterlily needs a warm-temperate climate to flower well. Purple-mottled when young, the leaves mature to plain green, round to oval pads, up to 8in/20cm across. The flowers are semidouble, with long yellow petals and yellow stamens. Depth 12–18in/30–45cm, spread 4–5ft/1.2–1.5m. ⬛ 🔲 Z10–11

Nymphaea tetragona

Nymphaea 'Virginia'

Nymphaea tetragona
Delightful white-flowered waterlily suitable for a small or container pond, best given protection over winter in Zones 4–6. The oval leaves are blotched with purple; the flowers are slightly fragrant. Depth 6–8in/15–22cm, spread 2–3ft/60cm–1m. ⬛ 🔲 Z7–11

Nymphaea 'Virginia'
Free-flowering, with purplish green leaves and star-shaped, semidouble, pale yellow (near white) flowers, 4–6in/10–15cm across and star-shaped, with narrow, chrysanthemum-like petals. Depth 12–18in/30–45cm, spread 5–6ft/1.5–2m. ⬛ 🔲 Z4–11

Nymphaea 'Wood's White Knight'
Vigorous, night-blooming, for a larger tropical or heated pond. The almost circular leaves, up to 16in/40cm across, have unusual scalloped edges. The large, narrow-petaled white flowers open wide around central yellow stamens. Depth 16–24in/40–60cm, spread 8–10ft/2.5–3m. ⬛ 🔲 Z10–11

LOTUSES

WITH THEIR STRIKING bluish green leaves, large midsummer flowers, and "showerhead" seedheads, lotuses (*Nelumbo*) are exceptionally beautiful water plants. Most require hot weather, although they do well in colder zones where summers are long and hot; alternatively, they make striking plants for a conservatory. Most do well in planting depths of 6–24in/15–60cm. The stout leaf stalks soon thrust the foliage into the air, up to 6ft/2m above water.

Nelumbo nucifera 'Momo Botan'

Deciduous perennial, smaller than most lotuses, needing water no deeper than 12in/30cm. The peonylike double flowers are rose-pink, with yellow at the petal bases. It has a longer flowering season than most lotuses, and the flowers also stay open for longer, sometimes all night. Height 2–4ft/60cm–1.2m, spread 3ft/1m. ▣ ▣ **Z4–11**

NELUMBO 'MOMO BOTAN'

Nelumbo nucifera 'Mrs. Perry D. Slocum'

Deciduous perennial with glaucous leaves. It is exceptionally free-flowering, the blooms in many ways resembling those of the rose 'Peace'. Petals change color as the flower develops: pink flushed yellow on the first day, pink and yellow on the second day, and cream flushed with pink on the third. Height 4–5ft/1.2–1.5m, spread indefinite. ▣ ▣ **Z4–11**

Nelumbo 'Shiroman' (syn. *N. nucifera* var. *alba plena*)

Vigorous deciduous perennial, with 2ft/60cm-diameter leaves. The slightly fragrant, large double flowers, 10in/25cm across, are creamy white in color, with golden stamens in the center. Rapidly spreading; only for a medium to large pond. Height 3–5ft/1–1.5m, spread indefinite. ▣ ▣ **Z4–11**

Nelumbo 'Perry's Giant Sunburst'

Deciduous perennial with blue-green leaves, 16–20in/

NELUMBO 'PERRY'S SUPER STAR'

40–50cm across. Pleasantly fragrant, large flowers, up to 14in/35cm in diameter, are a rich creamy color, with buttery yellow stamens. They are held well above the leaves on robust, erect stalks. Height 4½–5½ft/1.4–1.7m, spread indefinite. ▣ ▣ **Z4–11**

Nelumbo 'Perry's Super Star'

Deciduous perennial with blue-green leaves. The sweetly scented flowers change in hue as they develop, from rich pink to yellow, culminating in a creamy color, with pink petal tips. They are unusual in having six to eight green-tipped petals clustered at the center of the flower. Height 3–4ft/1–1.2m, spread indefinite. ▣ ▣ **Z4–11**

MARGINAL PLANTS

MARGINALS INHABIT SHALLOW WATER, usually around the edges of a pond. While most of their topgrowth is visible above the water surface, their bases and roots are under water. Many also grow well in permanently saturated soil. Their vertical presence contrasts well with the flat water surface and the leaves of floating plants, and it softens pond edges. It is important to position marginals in the depth of water that is appropriate for each individual plant.

Acorus calamus
(Myrtle flag, sweet flag)
Deciduous, rhizomatous perennial with irislike leaves (striped with cream in 'Variegatus') with wrinkled edges. Small, conical flowers emerge just below leaf tips. Divide in spring. H 30in/75cm, S 2ft/60cm, water depth to 10in/25cm. ▣ ▨ Z4–11

Alisma plantago-aquatica
(Water plantain)
Rhizomatous perennial with rosettes of oval leaves held on long stalks above water. Dainty, pinkish white flowers open in the summer. Self-seeds readily in wet soil; the seeds are also food for wildlife. Divide in spring. H 30in/75cm, S 18in/45cm, water depth to 10in/25cm. ▣ ▨♦ Z5–8

ERIOPHORUM ANGUSTIFOLIUM

Butomus umbellatus
(Flowering rush)
Perennial with bronze shoots that develop into thin, olive-green leaves. Rose-pink flowers are borne above the leaves on tall, cylindrical stems in summer. Best grown in open shallows; if containerized it needs regular dividing and repotting. H 2–4ft/60cm–1.2m, water depth 2–16in/5–40cm. ▣ ▨ Z5–11

Calla palustris (Bog arum)
Deciduous or semi-evergreen perennial with long, creeping rhizomatous roots. White, arumlike flower spathes appear in spring, followed by clusters of red or orange berries. Divide in spring. H 10in/25cm, S 12in/30cm, water depth to 2in/5cm. ▣ ▨ Z4–8

Caltha palustris
(Marsh marigold, kingcup)
Deciduous, hardy perennial that grows freely alongside streams and ditches in the northern hemisphere. In spring it produces clusters of waxy, cup-shaped, bright golden yellow flowers, held above smooth, deep green leaves. 'Flore Pleno' is double-flowered. Divide in spring or early autumn. H 2ft/60cm, S 18in/45cm, water depth to 6in/15cm. ▣ ▨♦ Z3–7

Cyperus
Evergreen, perennial sedges with stout, leafless stems, triangular in cross-section. Mop-head tufts of fine, pendulous leaves and rayed flower sprays in summer. *C. papyrus* (papyrus) is tender and not easy to grow, but *C. longus* is hardier (Zones 7–10). Shelter from wind. Divide in autumn. H 6–10ft/3–5m, S 3ft/1m, water depth to 10in/25cm. ▣ ▨ Hardiness varies

Eriophorum (Cotton grass)
Evergreen marsh or marginal plants forming dense tufts of grasslike leaves. Flowers form as white, downy "cotton balls." Best in acidic conditions, such as peaty soil. Divide in autumn. H 12–18in/30–45cm, S indefinite, water depth to 2in/5cm. ▣ ▨♦ Z4–7

ALISMA PLANTAGO-AQUATICA

Glyceria maxima
(Sweet grass, manna grass)
Deciduous, perennial aquatic grass; var. *variegata* has leaves striped with creamy white, often flushed pink at the base. Flowers are open heads of greenish spikelets in summer. Divide in autumn. H 3ft/1m, S indefinite, water depth to 6in/15cm. ◪ ▨◆ Z5–9

Juncus (Rushes)
Evergreen, tuft-forming perennial plants that grow well in shallow water or damp soil. The dark green,

JUNCUS EFFUSUS 'SPIRALIS'

leafless stems twist and curl intriguingly in *J. effusus* 'Spiralis', the corkscrew rush. Dense, greenish brown flower tufts form in summer. Divide in spring. H 2–3ft/60cm–1m, S 18–24in/45–60cm, water depth to 2in/5cm. ◪ ◪ ▨◆◆ Z4–9

Lysichiton (Skunk cabbage)
Vigorous, deciduous perennials with stout rhizomes, ideal for muddy shallows and tolerant of moving water. Callalike spathes surrounding erect

WATER IRISES

Sun-loving, deciduous perennials with strap-shaped leaves, flowers in shades of blue, purple, yellow, or white, and thick, fleshy roots (rhizomes); they grow well in planting baskets, restricting their spread in small ponds. Irises are useful linking plants to help the margins of a pool blend in with surrounding planting areas. Most can be grown either in shallow water or in damp soil; there are other irises to grow on moist but well-drained soil, such as *Iris sibirica* (*see p.75*), together with the garden irises that flourish in drier ground. Divide crowded clumps in late summer.

Iris ensata
Dense tufts of bold, sword-shaped leaves and blue or white flowers, 3–6in/8–15cm across. Dislikes lime. It is best lifted from the water and plunged, in its basket, in

garden soil for the winter. H 2–3ft/60cm–1m, S indefinite. ◪ ▨◆◆ Z5–8

Iris laevigata
Broad leaves, white-striped in 'Variegata', and mauve, white, or pink flowers in summer. H 2–3ft/60cm–1m, S indefinite, water depth to 4in/10cm. Can be grown in moist soil but must never dry out. ◪ ▨◆◆ Z4–9

IRIS ENSATA 'BLUE PETER'

Iris pseudacorus
(Yellow flag)
Robust, vigorous, with thick roots. The broad, ridged leaves are gray-green; those of 'Variegata' are striped with yellow. Each tall, branched stem can bear up to 10 flowers, usually golden to yellow in color with large fall petals that often have a dark patch in the center. H to 6ft/2m, S indefinite, water depth to 12in/30cm, or grow in wet or moist soil. ◪ ▨◆◆ Z5–8

Iris versicolor
(Blue flag, wild iris)
Clump-forming, with narrow, gray-green leaves. Each branched stem bears three to five violet-blue or lavender flowers, their fall petals white-veined with purple, yellow-blotched at the base. H 2ft/60cm, water depth to 2ft/60cm. Also grows in wet soil. ◪ ▨◆ Z3–9

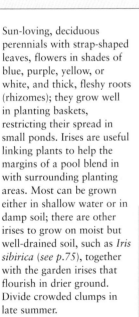

MENYANTHES TRIFOLIATA

ORONTIUM AQUATICUM

Orontium aquaticum
(Golden club)
Deciduous, rhizomatous
perennial tolerating fairly
deep water, on which the
leaves, bluish green with a
silvery sheen on the underside,
will float. The pokerlike
flowerheads stand well above
the water. Divide in spring.
H 12–18in/30–45cm,
S 2ft/60cm, water depth to
12in/30cm. ▨ ▨ ▨ Z6–11

Peltandra (Arrow arum)
Deciduous perennials with
arrow-shaped, bright green
leaves. Narrow, white or
green flower spathes,
sometimes yellow-edged,
appear in summer, followed
by red or green berries.
Divide in spring.
H 3ft/1m, S 2ft/60cm, water
depth 2–3in/5–7cm.
▨ ▨ Z5–11

Pontederia cordata
(Pickerel weed)
Robust, deciduous perennial
that forms dense clumps of
slender stems bearing smooth,
narrowly heart-shaped leaves.
In late summer, compact
spikes of soft blue flowers

spikes of small flowers appear
in early spring, before the
bright green, paddlelike,
leathery leaves. The flowers
are yellow in *L. americanus*,
white in *L. camschatcensis*.
H 30in/75cm, S 2–3ft/
60cm–1m, water depth
1in/2.5cm. ▨ ▨♦♦ Z7–9

Mentha aquatica
(Water mint)
Low-growing, spreading
perennial with fresh green
leaves, fragrant when crushed.
The creeping roots are useful
for binding wet soil together.
In summer, it bears delicate
clusters of flowerheads in a
faded rose-pink. Like all
mints, it spreads rapidly and
should be thinned if it
encroaches on other plants.
Divide in spring or autumn.
H 6in/15cm, S indefinite,
water depth 6in/15cm.
▨ ▨♦ Z6–9

Menyanthes trifoliata
(Bog bean, buckbean,
marsh trefoil)
Deciduous perennial; three-
lobed, olive green leaves held
on tall, sheathed stalks. Dainty,
white to purplish flowers open

from pink buds in late spring.
Divide early spring. H 10in/
25cm, S indefinite, water
depth 2in/5cm. ▨ ▨ Z3–7

Myosotis scorpioides
(Water forget-me-not)
Perennial with creeping roots.
Stems are first prostrate, then
erect, forming sprawling
mounds of narrow, mid-green
leaves. Flowers early- to midsummer; clusters of small, blue
flowers have a central eye of
pink, yellow, or white.
H 6–9in/15–22cm, S 12in/
30cm, water depth 6in/15cm.
▨ ▨♦ Z5–9

RANUNCULUS LINGUA

PONTEDERIA CORDATA

SAGITTARIA LATIFOLIA

TYPHA LATIFOLIA

develop from within a leaf at the stem tip. Divide in spring. H 30in/75cm, S 18in/45cm, water depth 5in/12cm. ☐ ☑ **Z3–11**

Ranunculus
There are only two aquatic buttercups, both deciduous perennials that flower in late spring. *R. lingua* has golden yellow flowers that are held high above the water ('Grandiflora' has the largest); *R. aquatilis* grows mostly underwater, with floating flowers, white with yellow centers. Divide in spring. H (*R. lingua*) to 5ft/1.5m, S 6ft/2m, water depth 3–6in/7–15cm. ☐ ☑ **Z4–9**

Sagittaria (Arrowhead)
Deciduous perennials with lance-shaped, soft green leaf-blades and whorls of tall-stalked, 3-petaled white flowers in summer. They develop tubers at the ends of creeping subterranean stems that may be separated from the parent to grow on as new plants. H to 4ft/1.2m, S 2ft/60cm, water depth 6in/15cm. ☐ ☑ **Z5–11**

Schoenoplectus lacustris subsp. *tabernaemontani*
Perennial, spreading rush with tough, creeping rhizomes. This subspecies is half the height of the towering species, yet still needs a largish pond. The stems of 'Zebrinus' have horizontal cream banding. Flowers are white and brown, in spikes, in summer. Divide in spring. H 5ft/1.5m, S indefinite, water depth 3–6in/7–15cm. ☐ ☑ **Z4–8**

Scrophularia auriculata
(Water figwort)
Coarse-leaved evergreen for shallows or moist soil. 'Variegata' has cream-edged foliage. The greenish flowers, popular with bees, should be removed to prevent self-seeding. Divide in summer. H 3ft/1m, S 2ft/60cm, water depth 3in/7cm. ☐ ☑ **Z5–9**

Typha (Cattail)
Deciduous, perennial plants for shallow water or wet soil. *Typha latifolia* forms large clumps of wide leaves, cream-striped in 'Variegata', with cylindrical tail-like heads. *T. minima* is smaller, forming slender tufts; its brown flower spikes mature into cylindrical seedheads. Divide in spring. *T. latifolia*: H 3–4ft/1–1.2m, S indefinite, water depth to 10in/25cm. ☐ ☑ **Z3–11**. *T. minima*: H 2ft/60cm, S 12in/30cm, planting depth to 6in/15cm. ☑ ☑ **Z3–11**

Veronica beccabunga
(Brooklime)
Semi-evergreen scrambling perennial with white-centered blue flowers and fleshy, creeping, rooting stems. Divide in autumn; replace old straggly specimens. H 4in/10cm, S indefinite, water depth 3in/7cm. ☐ ☑ **Z5–11**

Zantedeschia aethiopica
(Calla lily)
Tuberous plants, fairly hardy under water, ideal in a formal setting. Dark, glossy leaves and, in summer, large, fragrant flower spathes, pure white in 'Crowborough' and splashed green in 'Green Goddess', with yellow spikes. Divide mature plants late winter. H 18–36in/45cm–1m, S 14–24in/35–60cm, water depth to 12in/30cm. ☐ ☑◊ **Z7–10**

VERONICA BECCABUNGA

MOISTURE-LOVING PLANTS

THERE IS A WIDE RANGE OF PLANTS that not only tolerate but positively thrive in moist soil. They include not only those plants seen growing naturally by streams and poolsides but also many that, although traditionally grown in more normal garden soil conditions, will excel in this fringe environment. While boggy soil saturated with water is ideal for many marginal plants, nearly all moisture-lovers need good drainage and will not tolerate waterlogging.

AJUGA REPTANS 'MULTICOLOR'

Ajuga reptans (Bugle)
Evergreen perennial whose stems spread and root to form a creeping mat. Blue spring flowers with purple bracts are carried on spikes 4–5in/10–13cm high above leaves that are often attractively patterned and colored. Divide or detach rooted portions in spring. H 4–5in/10–13cm, S indefinite. ▣▣ ◊ Z3–9

Astilbe
Herbaceous perennials forming clumps of divided leaves, with plumelike flowerheads on tall stems in summer, in white, cream, red, or shades of pink, remaining attractive when brown in autumn. Divide in early spring. H 18–24in/45–60cm, S 14–20in/35–50cm. ▣▣ ◊ Z4–9

Carex (Sedges)
Perennial plants with grasslike leaves, several with variegated or colored foliage; that of *C. elata* 'Aurea' is a bright gold. Tall stems support graceful brown flower spikes, arching in *C. pendula*, which is striking reflected in a still pool. Some also grow well in very shallow water. Divide in spring. H 2–3ft/60cm–1m, S 18in/45cm. ▣▣ ◊◊ Z3–9

Chelone obliqua
(Turtle head, shellflower)
Herbaceous perennial with upright stems supporting serrated dark green leaves. In late summer and autumn it produces purple or white penstemon-like flowers. Divide in spring or autumn. H 3ft/1m, S 20in/50cm. ▣ ◊ Z5–9

CAREX PENDULA

Cimicifuga simplex
Herbaceous perennial that thrives in damp, light shade. The flowers, white or pale pink, are slightly fragrant, held in delicate spikes on dark, wiry stems; may need staking in open sites. 'Brunette' has purple foliage. 'Elstead' is one of the last to flower, sometimes well into late autumn. Divide in spring. H 4ft/1.2m, S 18in/45cm. ▣ ◊ Z4–8

Dryopteris filix-mas
(Male fern)
Deciduous or semi-evergreen fern, usually pleasingly well-shaped, with upright, then delicately arching mid-green fronds. Grows equally well either in moist or in well-drained but moisture-retentive soil, but prefers a shady site.

CHELONE OBLIQUA

EUPATORIUM PURPUREUM

Remove fading fronds. Divide in autumn or winter. H 3ft/1m, S 3ft/1m. ▨▨ ◊◊ **Z4–8**

Eupatorium purpureum
(Joe Pye weed)
Clump-forming perennial with purple-tinged, mid-green leaves, finely toothed and pointed, bearing pink or cream flowerheads from midsummer to early autumn. Prefers alkaline soil. H to 7ft/2.2m, S 3–5ft/1–1.5m. ▨▨ ◊ **Z3–9**

Filipendula
Herbaceous perennials with beautifully divided, fresh green

FILIPENDULA ULMARIA 'AUREA'

leaves (young foliage is golden green in *F. ulmaria* 'Aurea'). Branching heads of pink or creamy flowers are carried in midsummer. Deadhead to encourage new growth. Divide in autumn. H 2ft/60cm, S 18in/45cm. ▨ ◊◊ **Z3–9**

Hosta (Plantain lily)
Herbaceous, clump-forming perennials grown for their large, attractive leaves, fresh green to blue-gray, many splashed or edged with white or cream. Gray-white or pale violet, trumpet-shaped flowers held above foliage on graceful stalks in midsummer. Divide in spring, only if new plants are wanted. H 30in/75cm, S to 3ft/1m. ▨ ◊◊ **Z3–8**

Iris sibirica (Siberian iris)
Rhizomatous perennial with upright sheaves of grasslike leaves. Each stem bears two or three dark-veined blue or blue-purple flowers (white in var. *alba*), 2–4in/5–10cm across. An adaptable plant that will also flourish in drier soil. Divide in late summer. H 18in/45cm, S 3ft/1m. ▨ ◊◊ **Z4–9**

Kirengeshoma palmata
Erect herbaceous perennial forming clumps of large, rounded leaves, hairy on both sides, with irregularly cut edges. The funnel-shaped flowers, pale yellow and waxen, hang in loose sprays on purplish stems in late summer. Dislikes lime. Divide in autumn or spring. H 3ft/1m, S 2ft/60cm. ▨ ◊◊ **Z5–8**

Liatris spicata (Gayfeather)
Herbaceous perennial with swollen, flattened stems and narrow leaves. The densely

HOSTA 'FORTUNEI AUREOMARGINATA'

clustered, thick flower spikes, in pink, white or, in 'Kobold', rich purple, open from the top downward over a long period in late summer to early autumn; they are attractive to bees. H 5ft/1.5m, S 18in/45cm. ▨▨ ◊ **Z4–9**

Ligularia
Clump-forming, herbaceous perennials with large, richly veined, deep green leaves. In mid- to late summer, daisy-like, yellow or orange flowers open in large, pyramidal spikes. Tend to wilt quickly on bright, windy days or in dry spells. Divide in spring. H 6ft/2m, S 2ft/60cm. ▨ ◊ **Z4–8**

Lobelia
Medium-height, clump-forming perennials in this genus, such as *L. cardinalis*, are very different from bedding lobelias, thriving in moist soil. They have upright stems of lance-shaped leaves, either fresh green or purple-bronze in plants such as 'Queen Victoria', and tall spikes of two-lipped, purple, blue, or scarlet flowers from

mid- to late summer. Dislike excess winter moisture; if the site gets boggy, move them to drier ground over winter. Divide in spring. H 3ft/1m, S 10in/25cm. Z3–9

Matteuccia struthiopteris
(Ostrich fern)
Deciduous, rhizomatous fern that can be grown in ordinary garden conditions or in moist ground. Dark brown inner fronds stand erect, surrounded by a green "shuttlecock" of spreading outer fronds. Divide in autumn or winter. H 3ft/1m, S 18in/45cm. Z3–8

Mimulus cardinalis
(Scarlet monkey flower)
Branching perennial with, from midsummer onward, sprays of bright red, snapdragon-like flowers. It can become messy in late summer and should be cut back to prompt new growth. Divide in spring, or grow as an annual where winters are severe. H 2–3ft/60cm–1m, S 3ft/1m. Z6–9

OSMUNDA REGALIS

Osmunda regalis
(Royal fern)
Elegant, deciduous fern. Mature plants bear sterile fronds to 6ft/2m high, in a pale, copper-tinted green that deepens to rich green. Pale brown, fertile flower spikes appear at the tips of taller fronds. Protect the base with a mulch in winter. Divide in winter. H 6ft/2m, S 3ft/1m. Z4–9

Parnassia palustris
(Grass of Parnassus)
Small perennial, often evergreen, forming low tufts of heart-shaped, pale or mid-green leaves. Buttercup-like white flowers, with dark green or purplish green veins, borne on erect stems late spring and early summer. H 8in/20cm, S 4in/10cm. Z4–11

POOLSIDE PRIMROSES

All primroses look good by an informal pool, and the upright-stemmed candelabra and drumstick types also fit a formal setting. The hardy moisture-lovers here are all small, clump-forming perennials, flowering in early to mid-summer, forming basal rosettes of leaves around upright flower stems. They have a tendency to spread by self-seeding. H 12–24in/30–60cm, S 12–18in/30–45cm. Z3–8

Primula beesiana
Compact candelabra type with leaves that are white-powdered below, and rose-purple flowers with a yellow eye.

Primula bulleyana
Long-lasting heads of flowers are deep orange, or sometimes mauve.

Primula florindae
The giant cowslip, with loose heads of drooping, powdery yellow flowers. Ideal for a wildlife pond.

Primula japonica
Stout stems bear tiers of flowers, available in shades of pink, red-purple, and white; many are eyed.

Primula prolifera
Vigorous, with stout stems bearing dense whorls of bright yellow flowers, excellent planted *en masse*.

PRIMULA BULLEYANA

Primula pulverulenta
Candelabra type with loose heads of dainty flowers, red or red-purple or, in 'Bartley', shell pink with dark eyes.

PARNASSIA PALUSTRIS

Persicaria bistorta
Vigorous, clump-forming, herbaceous perennial with dense, docklike basal foliage. Erect, broad, bottlebrush-like spikes of soft pink flowers are produced over a long period; 'Superba' is very persistent. Can become invasive; divide spring or autumn. H 24–30in/60–75cm, S 2ft/60cm. ⬛ ◊◊ **Z4–8**

Phlox paniculata
This phlox does well in moist soil, as long as it is not limy or clayey. It is an upright herbaceous perennial with attractive foliage; in 'Norah Leigh', leaves are cream with a thin, central zone of green. Pyramidal heads of fragrant mauve, pale pink or white flowers open in summer. Divide in spring. H and S 2ft/60cm. ⬛ ◊ **Z4–8**

Rheum palmatum
Stout, clump-forming perennial grown for its large, deeply cut leaves; those of 'Atrosanguineum' are rich red-purple when young, retaining this color on the undersides in maturity. Dense

spikes of small, rusty red flowers appear in early summer. Grows best in deep, moist soil. Divide in spring. H and S 6ft/2m. ⬛ ◊ **Z5–9**

Rodgersia pinnata
Rhizomatous perennial forming clumps of large, emerald green, sometimes bronze-tinged leaves. Plumes or clusters of pink or white flowers appear in summer. Well suited to a woodland setting. Divide in spring. H 3–4ft/1–1.2m, S 3ft/1m. ⬛ ◊ **Z5–8**

Salix (Willow)
Most willows flourish in moist soil: smaller, shrubby types that look well in poolside plantings include *S. hastata* 'Wehrhahnii', a deciduous shrub for free-draining or moist soil. White catkins are borne on polished stems in early spring, before the oval green leaves appear. H and S 5ft/1.5m. ⬛ ◊◊ **Z2–9**

Thelypteris palustris
(Marsh fern)
Deciduous fern with long, creeping roots and deeply divided, long-stalked, pale green fronds. Fertile fronds are produced only in good light. Their prolific, tiny fruiting bodies may produce a brown haze over plants in late summer. H 2ft/60cm, S 3ft/1m. ⬛ ◊ **Z5–8**

Tricyrtis macrantha
(Toad lily)
Tufted, herbaceous perennial with thick rhizomes and arching or prostrate brown, hairy stems. Glossy, dark green leaves are heart-shaped at the base. In early and mid-autumn,

long, bell-shaped, pendulous, deep yellow flowers, spotted red-brown inside, with thick, fleshy petals develop from the upper leaf axils. Divide in early spring, before growth begins. H 16–32in/40–80cm, S 12in/30cm. ⬛✳ ◊ **Z8–9**

Trillium
Clump-forming perennials with mid-green leaves borne in whorls of three. White or maroon-purple three-petaled flowers borne in spring, some unpleasant-smelling (such as those of *T. erectum*, stinking Benjamin) but attractive. Divide in late summer. H 10–18in/25–45cm, S 8–12in/20–30cm. ⬛✳ ◊ **Z5–9**

Trollius (Globeflower)
Compact perennials with flowers resembling large, usually double buttercups, with thick, fibrous roots and rounded, divided, mid-green leaves. Solitary, globe-shaped, lemon to mid-yellow flowers are borne on tall, slender stems in spring. Divide in early autumn. H 20–24in/50–60cm, S 14–18in/35–45cm. ⬛⬛ ◊ **Z5–8**

TROLLIUS EUROPAEUS

INDEX

ACKNOWLEDGMENTS

Picture research Mollie Gillard
Special photography Peter Anderson
Illustrations Karen Cochrane
Index Hilary Bird

DK Publishing would like to thank:
All staff at the Royal Horticultural Society, in particular Susanne Mitchell, Karen Wilson, and Barbara Haynes at Vincent Square.

Photography
The publisher would also like to thank the following for their kind permission to reproduce their photographs:
(key: t=top, c=center, b=below, l=left, r=right)

AKG London: 7cr
A–Z Botanical Collection: Andrew Cowin 62, Michael R. Chandler 6tc, Neil Joy 6bc
The Garden Picture Library: back cover tr, 10, Brian Carter 5bl, 67tr; Howard Rice 21c, John Glover 27cb; Lamontagne 6; Sunniva Harte 21cl; Vaughan Flemming 14bl
Garden Matters: 31cr, 64tl

John Glover: 13t, 22, 27cr, 32cr, 32cr, 34, 42tr
Robert Harding Syndication: Hugh Palmer/*Homes & Gardens* 16
Jerry Harpur: 8tr
Andrew Lawson: front cover tl, 2, 11b, 13br
Clive Nichols: front cover cl, 12, 14br, 15, 28, 38tr
Oxford Scientific Films: P. K. Sharpe 63bc
Photos Horticultural: 8bl, 9tr, Birt Association of Landscape Industries 52bl; Michael & Lois Warren front cover c, 4br, 48
Harry Smith Collection: 7bl, 67bl
Stapeley Water Gardens: 68bc
Elizabeth Whiting & Associates: 11tr

American Horticultural Society
Visit AHS at www.ahs.org or call them at 1-800-777-7931 ext.10. Membership benefits include *The American Gardener* magazine, free admission to flower shows, the free seed exchange, book services, and the Gardener's Information Service.